Dear Future Exam Success Story

First of all, **THANK YOU** for purchasing Mometrix study materials!

Second, congratulations! You are one of the few determined test-takers who are committed to doing whatever it takes to excel on your exam. **You have come to the right place.** We developed these study materials with one goal in mind: to deliver you the information you need in a format that's concise and easy to use.

In addition to optimizing your guide for the content of the test, we've outlined our recommended steps for breaking down the preparation process into small, attainable goals so you can make sure you stay on track.

We've also analyzed the entire test-taking process, identifying the most common pitfalls and showing how you can overcome them and be ready for any curveball the test throws you.

Standardized testing is one of the biggest obstacles on your road to success, which only increases the importance of doing well in the high-pressure, high-stakes environment of test day. Your results on this test could have a significant impact on your future, and this guide provides the information and practical advice to help you achieve your full potential on test day.

Your success is our success

We would love to hear from you! If you would like to share the story of your exam success or if you have any questions or comments in regard to our products, please contact us at **800-673-8175** or **support@mometrix.com**.

Thanks again for your business and we wish you continued success!

Sincerely,
The Mometrix Test Preparation Team

I0878840

Need more help? Check out our flashcards at:
http://mometrixflashcards.com/TExES

Mometrix
TEST PREPARATION

TExES

Computer Science 8-12 (241) Secrets Study Guide

TABLE OF CONTENTS

Programming Language Topics

Operators, Data Types, and Variables

Boolean Algebra vs. Standard Algebra

One of the main differences between standard algebra and Boolean algebra is the fact that standard algebra uses variables to represent numbers, whereas Boolean algebra uses variables to represent true or false values. Just as standard algebra follows certain rules, Boolean algebra also has a set of rules that must be applied. While standard algebra uses arithmetic operators like addition and subtraction, Boolean algebra uses logical operators like AND and OR. Boolean algebra can be used to prove the equivalence of propositional statements, just as standard algebra can be used to prove the equivalence of mathematical expressions.

De Morgan's Laws and Propositional Logic

De Morgan's laws are two expressions of one principle. They are important to propositional logic because they provide rules on which inferences can be based. They allow unions and intersections of sets to be expressed in terms of each other through the use of the negation operator. The laws read as follows: "The complement of the union of two sets is the same as the intersection of their complements, and the complement of the intersection of two sets is the same as the union of their complements." In terms of propositional logic, it may be easier to understand these laws expressed as logical statements:

NOT (A OR B) = (NOT A) AND (NOT B)
NOT (A AND B) = (NOT A) OR (NOT B)

Their application in Boolean algebra and working with sets is generally easiest to comprehend by seeing the laws expressed with Venn diagrams.

Venn Diagrams of De Morgan's Laws

De Morgan's laws can be represented with **Venn diagrams**. In each case, the resultant set is the set of all points in light blue (light gray for print readers).

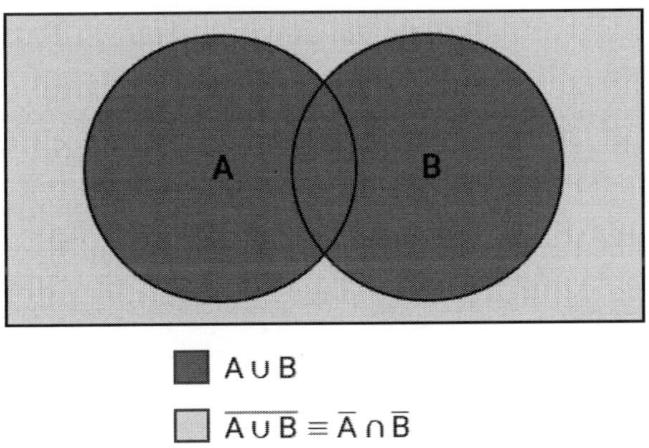

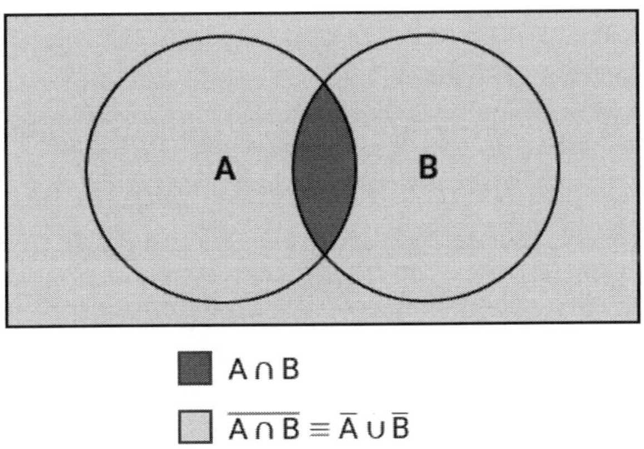

Example

A student is writing a program but doesn't remember what the AND operator is in the current programming language. The student decides to try to express (NOT A) AND (NOT B) without using AND, where A and B are Boolean variables. Write the logical expression that the student should use.

In order to solve this problem, we should remember De Morgan's laws. These laws provide equivalent Boolean expressions, including those that the student need. Recall that these laws can be stated in logical expressions as:

NOT (A OR B) = (NOT A) AND (NOT B)
NOT (A AND B) = (NOT A) OR (NOT B)

Therefore, the student can write NOT (A OR B) instead of (NOT A) AND (NOT B).

Including Arithmetic Functionality in Code

The inclusion of arithmetic functionality is actually quite simple because, in most cases, mathematical operators are already included in the programming language. Nearly every language that programmers would code in has basic arithmetic functionality built in. There is no need to identify or include any additional libraries or routines. A programmer can write mathematical expressions directly in code, as long as they follow the syntax of the language. In many cases, more advanced mathematical functions can be used as well by including a math library, which is a library of functions that are not included in a program by default, but that can be included using a statement.

Basic Arithmetic Operators

Arithmetic operators perform very basic mathematical calculations. Most of these require little or no explanation. These include addition, subtraction, multiplication, and division. Another operator included in most languages is the **modulo operator**. This operator returns the remainder of integer division rather than the whole number quotient. For example, 6 "mod" 3 is 0, because 6 divided by 3 is 2 with a 0 remainder. However, 7 mod 3 would be 1, because there is a remainder of 1 when this division is performed. Most arithmetic operators perform their operation on two values, given on either side, called operands. In the code `7 % 3`, the modulo operator `%` will perform its operation using the operands 7 and 3. More complex mathematical calculations, like square root, sine, and cosine, are not considered arithmetic operators.

Order of Operations

The **order of operations** used in most programming languages is the same as the order of operations used in mathematics. Some people use the mnemonic "PEMDAS" to help themselves remember the correct order. This stands for "parentheses, exponents, multiplication, division, addition, subtraction," which states the order in which arithmetic operations will be performed. The first operation that will be performed is any operation inside parentheses. Some expressions even contain multiple sets of parentheses as well as parentheses inside other parentheses to ensure that specific actions are carried out first. Next, any exponents will be evaluated, followed by multiplication and division, and finally, addition and subtraction.

It is important to remember that in math generally, as well as in most programming languages and software, multiplication and division share the same level of priority, and addition and subtraction share a lower level of priority. If an expression contains one use of multiplication and one use of division, these will be processed from left to right in most cases—meaning that the multiplication may be done after the division. For example, the code `10 / 5 * 2` will result in the division being done first and the multiplication second, yielding 4.

Code Example

Express the result obtained from the expression `2 * 2 + 1` *and identify a way to change the expression to obtain a different result.*

The result of this expression is 5. This is due to the order of operations, in which multiplication is performed before addition. The first operation to be performed is 2 times 2. This yields a result of 4. The addition 4 plus 1 is then performed, which generates the result of 5. By adding parentheses, a different result could be obtained. Examine the same expression with parentheses added:

```
2 * (2 + 1)
```

In this case, the operation inside the parentheses, 2 plus 1, will be performed first, yielding 3. Then the multiplication will be carried out, with 2 times 3 producing 6.

Importance of the Order of Operations

The order of operations is very important when evaluating mathematical expressions because, depending on the order of operations, the resulting value may be different. For example, look at the expression `2 + 3 * 2 + 4`. As written, this expression would produce a result of 12 in most programming languages. Due to the order of operations, the multiplication 3 times 2 would be performed first, then the addition 2 plus 6, and then finally 8 plus 4. However, the expression could have been carelessly written and intended to be evaluated left to right—2 plus 3 first, then 5 times 2, then 10 plus 4, yielding 14. Furthermore, the programmer could have wanted to perform the calculation `(2 + 3) * (2 + 4)`. In wanting to avoid left-to-right evaluation but confusing the order of operator priority, they could have written an expression where the multiplication would be done first rather than last, though last was intended. In many cases, developers may add parentheses as reassurance that an order will be followed or as a way of structuring an expression visually so as to make it more readable.

Operator Precedence

In the absence of parentheses, **operator precedence** determines the order in which a computer evaluates program expressions. This order, from highest to lowest, is as follows:

1. **Exponentiation**, or numbers that have been raised to a certain power
2. **Multiplication** and division in the order in which they appear from left to right
3. **Addition** and subtraction in the order in which they appear from left to right

When parentheses are present, they are evaluated before any other expression. The innermost parentheses are evaluated before the outermost parentheses, and the expressions inside parentheses are evaluated in the order of operator precedence. For instance, consider the following expression:

```
100 / (A * (B - C))
```

First, the computer would deal with parentheses. Finding that the outer set of parentheses has another set of parentheses inside it, the computer would evaluate `B - C`, the expression inside these inner parentheses. Then, it would multiply the resulting value by `A`. Finally, it will divide 100 by the resulting value.

In most programming languages, other operators figure into operator procedence as well. Examples of such operators include logical operators, like `AND` and `OR`, and unary operators (operators that use only one operand) like `++` and `--`. Programmers are well-served to be aware of operator precedence, to know when to double-check operator precedence, and know how or where to double-check it.

Relationship of Syntax Rules to Mathematical Expressions

Mathematical expressions must follow certain syntax rules. Operators must be in the correct place, and the correct number of inputs, or operands, must be provided. If these syntax rules are not followed, then an error will be produced. If the code must be compiled, the compiler will generate a syntax error that must be corrected before the code can run. Examples of valid expressions are as follows:

```
2 + 3 + 5 - 7
2 * 3 + 4 - 1
```

Remember that expressions may also include variables, such as:

```
2 * x + (a / 5)
```

An example of an invalid expression is:

```
3(4 + 8 -
```

Note that there is no closing parenthesis in the above expression, and that the subtraction operator is missing an input. This expression would generate a syntax error.

Data Types

Data types are categories for data. In computing, data is stored in memory as binary code, and data types provide a way for one kind of data (for example, integers) to have its own rules for being stored in memory and operated on, as compared to another kind of data (for example, text). Common data types include real numbers, Boolean variables, integers, characters, alphanumeric strings, and floating-point numbers. The data type determines the possible operations within a value set, the possible values within the set, and the storage method for the set. Data types also place constraints on the interpretation of data within a system and thereby enable the system to evaluate the correctness of computer algorithms. All programming languages incorporate data types—though the terminology may differ from language to language. Often, programmers may also create their own data types and associated operations. In most cases, new data types combine characteristics of existing data types.

Integer Data Type

Just as in mathematics, an **integer** in computing is a positive or negative whole number. Many languages refer to it as an **int**. Fractions or decimals cannot be included as part of an integer. The range of integers that can be used depends on the amount of memory or storage size for the integer itself. Typically, an integer is allocated either 2 or 4 bytes for storage. The use of 2 bytes allows for a range of integers from –32,768 up to 32,767. Increasing the storage to 4 bytes drastically increases the range. Using 4 bytes allows for the use of integers from roughly negative 2 billion up to positive 2 billion. Some examples of integers are 3, 24, –67, and 1431. Numbers that are not considered integers include those with values to the right of the decimal point, such as 2.5, and "mixed numbers" (or numbers with fractions) such as 12 ½.

Floating-Point Data Type

The floating-point data type, or simply **float**, is used to represent numbers that have a decimal component. This could also include numbers with fractions, though the fractions would be represented in a decimal format. If there is any chance that calculations performed during the running of the program could lead to a result that includes a decimal point, then a floating-point type should be used to avoid losing the data after the decimal point. Some languages may also include a floating-point type called a **double**. Such a data type is used to represent a floating-point number with more precision. To accomplish the higher precision, languages allocate more memory for doubles—often double the amount of memory, and thus the name "double." Thanks to the additional memory, double can store many more **significant digits**. In other words, they store numbers that are more precise because there can be more digits on either side of the decimal point. Examples of floating-point numbers include 3.14, 6.73, and 1.25368474.

Boolean Data Type

The Boolean data type, or simply **bool**, has only two possible values: "true" and "false." Some languages actually store the words "true" and "false" to represent a Boolean value, while others may use the number 1 (usually to indicate "true") and the number 0 (usually to indicate "false"). It should be noted that not every programming language explicitly contains a Boolean data type. Boolean data types are generally used in logical expressions, and when logical operators (such as AND) or relational operators (such as ==) are used, they usually return a value of the Boolean data type. For instance, in the conditional test `7 > 5`, the "greater than" operator would return the Boolean value "true," while `3 == 6` would return the Boolean value "false." In programming, this type of logic is used very frequently to allow the program to make decisions during its processing. For example, in many languages, an if statement checks for the Boolean value "true," while the operators in the condition itself provide this value. Even languages that do not explicitly include a Boolean data type still allow for this kind of conditional testing.

String Data Type

The **string data type** is used to store text. Information that is considered "text" in this case includes not only letters and numerals, but also spaces, non-alphanumeric characters (such as punctuation), symbols or special characters, and formatting characters such as line breaks. Strings are often stored as arrays of characters, with each character occupying one position in the array. There are many operations that can be performed on strings. Some examples include concatenation, splitting, and joining. String parsing is another function that is commonly performed. This involves searching through a string to find desired text by looking for known text that occurs before or after the text that is needed. Some examples of strings include "string," "this is a string," and "Strings can even be complete sentences." When a string value (like "this is a string") is written in code, it generally needs to be set off with characters such as double quotation marks, so that the compiler does not try to interpret it as a function or variable. Remember that when strings are joined, spaces must be accounted for. For example, joining the strings "join" and "string" results in the string "joinstring." If a space is needed, it must be added as well.

Character Data Type

A **character data type** (often written as **char**) is, as its name suggests, a single character. The character may be a letter, number, or any other single piece of text. In most programming languages, the character data type is not used very often. Furthermore, some languages use an implementation of the character data type where a character is either a fixed-length string or a variable-length string. In languages that treat a character type as one single character, multiple characters may be joined together to create a string.

PRIMITIVE DATA TYPES

Primitive data types are the building blocks for all other types of data structures. A primitive data type is a basic data type which only holds values of one kind. Some examples include integers, characters, and Booleans. For example, the integer data type is primitive because it holds a single value that can only be an integer. That integer may be 2, –5, 91, or –23,545, but it will never be anything other than an integer. A character data type is primitive for the same reason. A variable of that data type will never hold anything other than one single character value. Depending on the language, there are generally somewhere between four and eight primitive character types. The most common types are integer, character, Boolean, and floating point.

SPEED OF PRIMITIVE DATA TYPE OPERATIONS

Operations on primitive data types run very quickly because primitive data types are relatively small, with most only requiring two to four bytes of memory. Because the value stored requires only this low number of bytes, there can be a one-to-one relationship between variables and blocks of memory. Therefore, data can be managed and accessed very quickly. Their small size also means primitive data types require a low number of CPU operations, sometimes as little as a single operation—and modern CPUs can run billions of operations every second. In summary, operations on primitive data types run very quickly because these data types require minimal memory, basic units of memory, and minimal processing power.

REFERENCE DATA TYPE

Reference data types can be a bit tricky for a new developer to understand. Reference data types contain information about a location in memory (i.e., a **memory address**) rather than the data itself. Consider the string "This is a string." If strings in this programming language are a reference data type, the string variable does not actually contain the value "This is a string." Rather, that value is stored in some location in memory. The string variable instead stores the address of this memory location. When the value of the string is needed, then the system goes to this location in memory and pulls the value from that location.

PRIMITIVE VS. REFERENCE DATA TYPES

One of the main differences between primitive and reference data types is the size and physical location of the data that is being dealt with. Primitive data types are small, often either two or four bytes. These data types can be stored completely within the **register** of the CPU. This is one reason why operations on primitive data type operations can often be performed within a single cycle of the CPU. Reference data types, however, may contain much larger pieces of data. Because of this, a reference data type stores only a memory address, and the data itself must be stored somewhere in the computer's memory system.

OBJECT DATA TYPE

An **object data type** forms the very basis of object-oriented programming. Objects can contain large pieces of data. An object is a reference data type because it uses a reference to a location in memory rather than storing the entire value. Objects are so large that they even contain **routines**. These allow a developer to perform specific functions within the object itself, offering a way for the developer to manipulate the data inside the object. The developer can be confident that the results will be consistent because the functionality is built into the object, and it does not have to be written with separate code in the main program.

WHAT MAKES AN ITEM AN OBJECT DATA TYPE

An object data type allows for the storage of much larger pieces or collections of data than a traditional primitive data type. Primitive data types are typically single items, such as integers or characters. Object data types, however, are collections of data, such as lists or arrays. An object data type is not simply stored in a small, single space in memory. Rather, it occupies more space in memory and is accessed by reference. This means that the memory address of the first item in the object is the actual value, and that first item is linked to the other items in the collection. An object is also classified by the functions that may be performed on the items in the data collection. Each object data type has a set of specific functions that may be performed on that data.

Object Data Types vs. Abstract Data Types

Data types allow a computer program to operate on pieces of data differently depending on the intended use of each piece of data. Object and abstract data types both require some level of abstraction (i.e., both involve rules and operations that the user and developer do not directly observe or control). Most modern programming languages do not actually provide any real implementation of abstract data types. In fact, abstract data types are often considered more an academic concept than a real data type that can be implemented in code. Object data types, however, are implemented very frequently and are quite common in all modern programming languages.

Abstract Data Types

An **abstract data type**, or ADT, is a data type whose definition remains constant between different programming languages. In essence, when two or more programming languages use an ADT, they will have similar semantics for it. In other words, a few rules or implementation details regarding the data type may be different from language to language, but the overall concept of that data type will be the same, and the same operations will likely be available, and are even likely to be called the same thing. For example, one language may have an implementation of stacks that is slightly different from that in another language, but the stack will still be essentially the same data structure, and its associated operations, such as pushing and popping, will be available.

Common ADTs include stacks, queues, priority queues, strings, containers, lists, deques (double-ended queues), maps, multimaps, multisets, trees, and sets. ADTs are used to describe abstract algorithms in simple terms, assess data structures, categorize data structures, and provide formal descriptions for programming languages. Although they are mostly theoretical and conceptual constructs, ADTs do appear in formal specification language. They can be implemented in the form of modules that include procedures for ADT operation. As conceptual tools, ADTs are important in object-oriented programming languages.

Importance of Choosing the Correct Data Type

A computer can interpret what appears to be the same value very differently depending on what data type is used. Take for instance the value "14235" as a data type of integer. In this case, the value is treated as the number fourteen thousand two hundred thirty-five (14,235). A developer could perform mathematical operations on this value, such as addition or subtraction. Contrast this with the same value "14235" being represented as a string data type. In this case, the value would be treated as the characters one, four, two, three, and five. Mathematical operations could not be performed on this value. However, additional characters could be appended to the value, or some characters could be removed from the value. These are just a couple of examples of how a value that is read one way by humans can be read differently by computers according to its data type.

Variables

A **variable** is a single location in the computer's memory capable of storing one value. Variables are given names by the programmer, but the name is just a human-readable reference to a memory location. Such locations provide temporary storage for multiple types of data, including numbers and characters. Program algorithms will later take values for variables in as inputs, process them, and generate output. There are two broad classifications for variables:

- **Global variables**: These are considered "in scope" throughout the entire program, including in functions and subroutines. In other words, any statement anywhere in the program can make use of these variables.
- **Local variables**: These are considered "in scope" only in part of the program, such as a specific function or subroutine. Only statements in the function where the variable is in scope may use these variables. For instance, if an integer variable were declared in both an object and a function which is defined inside of the object, and the programmer referenced the variable from within the function, the local copy of the variable (that is, the copy within function) would be that which is resolved, as it shares a scope with the code being executed. Variables belonging to objects can be referenced outside of those objects by specifically naming the object to which they belong, as long as they are not defined as private. Variables defined inside of functions or subroutines only exist while the method is executing. They are thus always inaccessible from outside of the method.

Scope

The **scope** of a variable defines sections of a program in which the variable exists, can be used, or can be known to exist. Scopes can nest programming elements or be nested within programming elements, and they contain various types of information, such as declarations, definitions of identifiers, and statements and expressions that define executable algorithms. The type of scope dictates program semantics, and the relationship between scope and semantics varies between programming languages. Scope also determines **information hiding**, which is the program's ability to "see" and access variables. Consider, for instance, a **namespace**, which is a type of scope that uses a single identifier to group several related identifiers logically. A variable declared within a procedure only exists within that procedure, and its scope is thus that procedure. Once the procedure has completed, the variable is destroyed. A variable that is a member of an object can share the same name as a variable that is a member of another object, as their scopes are different. For example, if ObjectA and ObjectB each have a variable named ObjName, then from within ObjectA, ObjName will resolve only to ObjectA's version, and likewise for ObjectB. However, if outside the scope of either of these objects, one has to reference the object in order to reference the variable (e.g., ObjectA.ObjName). ObjName is thus a **member** of ObjectA, and is limited by the scope of its parent (ObjectA). This allows a program to be organized logically and for common names to be reused without conflict.

How Variables Operate

The concept of a variable is a very important one to understand in programming. Without variables, developing anything other than very simple, single-use programs would be very difficult. Variables can be thought of as containers for values. Variables are given names so they can be easily identified by the programmer. Imagine needing to add two input numbers together and save the value for later use. You have no way of knowing what the sum will be until the program runs. Using a variable, you can store the sum and refer to it later in the code—and even name the variable `sum` to indicate what it contains. The value of `sum` may be different each time the program runs, but the program will still perform the same operations each time. Think of variables like containers into which values can be placed. When programs can be written to use these containers rather than constant values, programs can be used again and again without the need to manually change values in the code.

Constants vs. Variables

The difference between a variable and a constant is fairly straightforward. A variable is a placeholder for a value that can change at any time. Variables may change many times as a program runs. Constants, however, cannot change once they are established. A constant retains its original value throughout the entire running of the program. There are some cases where a constant is necessary because the developer may need to use a value that should never change. By using a constant, the developer can ensure that the value will stay the same throughout the entire program. In most programming, variables are used much more frequently than constants.

Lists

A **list** may sound simple in theory, but it can become quite complicated in its implementation. A list is a sequential grouping of data items that are all linked together. The specific details of the linking depend upon which type of list is being implemented. One of the most common implementations is a single **linked list**. In this type of list, each element within the list contains that element's value, as well as a **pointer** to the location of the next item in the list. There are a number of operations that can be performed on lists. Because lists can grow quite large, and because each item points to the memory location of the next item, a list is considered a reference data type.

Common Types of Lists

A list is a basic abstract data structure that arranges data entries sequentially. The first entry in a list is called the **head**, and the entry at the end is called the **tail**. Data in lists can generally be searched, rearranged, and changed. There are two basic types of lists: stacks and queues.

Stacks

One of the most common and simple abstract data types is a **stack**. Its name comes from the idea of a stack of trays, which serves as a metaphor for data retrieval. Each tray represents a data element. The last data saved is like a tray that is added to the stack at the top. Because it is added at the top, it will be the first tray taken off the stack when the time comes. Likewise, the last piece of data **pushed** onto the stack will be the first data returned (or **popped**) when the computer retrieves information from the stack. Stacks are known as "last in, first out" (**LIFO**) structures. Stack abstract data types perform two primary operations:

- **Push**: Occurs when a new data element is added to the stack
- **Pop**: Occurs when the computer retrieves the data that was saved most recently

Stacks can include any data type, including strings, integers, real numbers, pointers, and even other stacks. Because the operations of a stack are the same regardless of the programming language being used, it is considered an abstract data type.

In many cases, stacks provide the underlying structure for backtracking programs, which retrieve instructions in an order that is the reverse of the order in which they were entered. An example of backtracking is recursion. Recursion has many uses, but in one example, it could provide an "undo" operation, using a stack of executed commands, with the most recently executed instruction at the top. With this stack and a recursive algorithm, the commands could be undone in reverse order.

Queues

A **queue** is one of the most common abstract data types. It functions like a checkout line: The first person in the line will be the first person to leave the line. Likewise, in a queue retrieval system, the computer returns the first data element that was entered into the system. Consequently, a queue is known as a "first in, first out" (**FIFO**) structure. A queue performs the same two operations (push and pop) as a stack abstract data type (only with the pop function taking from the other end of the stack). The verb associated with entering data into a queue is "to enqueue." Similarly, that which pertains to the process of taking data out of the queue is "to dequeue." In many cases, queues provide the underlying structures for buffers, which store data temporarily for transfer between two locations.

Arrays

An **array** is a type of data structure. It contains elements that are identified using two features: the name of the array and the element's location within the array. Arrays can have any number of dimensions. The following is an example of an array with a single dimension:

```
int[] numberList ← {3,7,5,1}
```

The elements contained within this array are 3, 7, 5, and 1. If the system were asked to access one of them, it would identify both the name of the array, `numberList`, and the single integer that corresponds to the element's location. The location is identified with an index value, which in most cases starts with 0 and counts up for each member. By this system, the first member of the array `numberList` would be referred to as `numberList[0]`. As you can see, the other values are `numberList[1]`, which contains the value 7, `numberList[2]`, which contains the value 5, and `numberList[3]`, which contains the value 1.

Array Elements

All **elements** inside an array should be of the same data type due to the way that the computer stores an array in memory. Elements of the same data type each require the same amount of memory for storage, and this is critical to the storage and indexing of the array as a whole. When an array is stored in memory, the thing that is actually stored to represent the array is the memory address of the first item in the array. The system then allocates a specified amount of memory based on the size of the array and the data type of its members. For instance, consider an array of five integers, with each integer requiring four bytes of storage. The first item (element 0) in the array may be stored at memory address 2000, and the system would automatically place elements 1 through 4 in addresses 2004, 2008, 2012, and 2016. With each element requiring the same amount of memory, the computer can determine exactly where in memory any item in the array is located. If the members have different data types, therefore, the process is more complicated, as it cannot be assumed that the space allocated for each member will be equal, and the memory address for any given element would be unpredictable.

One-Dimensional Arrays vs. Multidimensional Arrays

A **one-dimensional** array is essentially a list in that it is just a series of similar data items constituting an array structure. **Multidimensional arrays**, however, are more like a list of lists; they have what can be thought of as rows and columns—two "dimensions." An array of this type may be referred to as a "table" or a "matrix." In order to reference a datapoint in a multidimensional array, the programmer needs an index value for each dimension—not just the one index value needed when dealing with a one-dimensional array. Consider the examples below.

2	4	6	8	10	12	14

If the above array were an int array called `list`, we could refer to the first number in the array with the term `list[0]`. The value stored in `list[0]` is the integer 2. We need only one index value because this array is one-dimensional.

A multidimensional array is a similar structure. However, for each additional dimension, another index value is needed to reference a specific datapoint. In the example below, two index values would be needed, because there are two dimensions:

2	4	6	8	10	12	14
4	6	8	10	12	14	16
6	8	10	12	14	16	18

If the above array were an int array called `table`, and if we are using a programming language in which the row index is written first, we could refer to the last value in the second row with the term `table[1][6]`. The value stored in `table[1][6]` is the integer 16.

For more dimensions, we would need more index values. In many programming languages it is possible to have a large number of dimensions in an array, but one-, two-, and three-dimensional arrays are most common.

Row-Major Order vs. Column-Major Order

Remember that a two-dimensional array looks like a matrix or a table. It has rows and columns. **Row-major order** and **column-major order** are two different techniques for storing the values of the array in memory. Programming languages handle this differently. If a language uses row-major order, the items in each row are stored consecutively, beginning at the first row. When the end of the first row is reached, the elements in the next row would then be stored, and so on. On the other hand, in column-major order, the contents of the first column are stored first, beginning from the top of the initial column. When the bottom of the first column is reached, the next column would then be stored, and so on. See the examples below for what the memory space may look like based on different ordering systems.

Sample array:

1	2	3	4
5	6	7	8
9	10	11	12

The series of memory addresses where the array is stored, if row-major order is used:

1	2	3	4	5	6	7	8	9	10	11	12

The series of memory addresses where the array is stored, if column-major order is used:

1	5	9	2	6	10	3	7	11	4	8	12

Multidimensional Arrays

A **multidimensional array** is a data structure that is also considered an array but is more complex than an array that has only one dimension or one index counter. When a system accesses elements in a multidimensional array, it identifies them using the array name and an index for each dimension. Consider the following multidimensional array:

```
int[][] numberTable ← {
    {1, 4, 8}
    {3, 7, 5}
    {2, 9, 0}
}
```

The elements contained within the array are 1, 4, 8, 3, 7, 5, 2, 9, and 0. If the system were asked to access one of them, it would identify both the array name, `numberTable`, and the two indices that correspond to the element's location. The first index is the row of the data element, and the second index is the column of data element. (In real life, we would need to know that the programming language we were working in followed this common convention.) Both indices count the members upward from 0. For instance, `numberTable[1][0]` identifies the 3 data element. Other elements include `numberTable[0][1]`, which is 4, and `numberTable[2][1]`, which is 9.

Homogenous Arrays

A **homogenous array** is a common type of abstract data structure in which all data must be the same data type (int, float, char, etc.). It can store a block of variables in either a one-dimensional list or a multidimensional array consisting of rows and columns. The program must declare the dimensions of the array. Consider the following example:

```
char Letters[][]
```

The above array is identified by the variable `Letters`. It will have four rows and five columns, and contain values of the char data type. Any time during the program's execution, code can refer to the array using its name or to a specific data element using the array's name along with an index or indices. An **index** is an integer value that identifies the position of a single element in the array. For instance, in FORTRAN language, the reference `Letter[1][1]` would identify the entry corresponding to the first row and first column. A programming language using the integer 1 to refer to the first element in an array is known as one-based indexing. In C, the same entry would be identified as `Letter[0][0]` because, in C, indices start at 0 rather than 1 (i.e., zero-based indexing).

Heterogeneous Arrays

A **heterogeneous array** is a common type of abstract data structure capable of storing different data types. Consider, for instance, a set of information containing the name of a product, its price, and the number of product units sold. This information could be stored in the following array:

```
String ProductName ← "Book IV"
float Price ← 29.95
int UnitsSold ← 2318
Object[] Params
Params[0] ← ProductName
Params[1] ← Price
Params[2] ← UnitsSold
```

`Object[]` declares a dynamic array named `Params`. In this case, it consists of three components: `ProductName`, which is a char data type; `Price`, which is a float data type; and `UnitsSold`, which is an int data type. The program can refer to the entire array using its name or to parts of the array using the array name, a period, and the component's name. An example of such a reference is `Product.UnitsSold`, which would evaluate to 2318.

Storing Data in Arrays vs. Variables

Using an array for data storage and manipulation has many advantages over using simple variables. First, the programmer can create many variables with one declaration statement instead of painstakingly declaring each variable individually. Second, passing data to methods is much easier when you must pass only one array of values rather than many individual values in separate variables. In this case, the array could also have any amount of data, and this amount would not have to be specified in the method header. Lastly, using a loop and an array is an easy and efficient way to move through data values, because it requires only a small amount of code. If the same data were contained in simple variables, loops could not be used as simply as with arrays, where the index value will change from one data item to the next.

Data Structures

A **data structure** contains a number of related variables. Using data structures, systems can process multiple variables at once. This ability is very useful when handling large amounts of data, such as customer lists, inventory lists, etc. A data structure would allow all this data to be grouped so that they can be processed efficiently. Procedural programming languages can handle a limited number of advanced data structures. Database systems can support the most advanced data structures.

One type of data structure is an array. It stores data in a list, where it can be accessed easily. Generally, an array contains values of only one data type. Procedural languages (such as C, FORTRAN, and COBOL) and object-oriented programming languages (such as C++ and Java) both make extensive use of arrays.

A data structure stores multiple related variables using a conceptual arrangement. Consider, for example, a day planner, which arranges information in a conceptual way. It consists of tables with rows and columns. Each page has a column to represent the day, and each row may represent an hour of the day. The entries in each table would list the activities planned for the corresponding day and time. Another example of a conceptual arrangement of data is a technical manual, which is divided into chapters, headings, subheadings, paragraphs, and sentences. Using data structures, systems can group variables together in a structure that corresponds to a real-life entity—a useful ability when a system must keep track of large amounts of data, such as every loyal shopper at a large retail store chain, every subject in a global study, or every item in a national system of warehouses and shipping vehicles. Types of data structures include lists, stacks, queues, trees, and arrays. Procedural languages such as FORTRAN and COBOL support a limited number of advanced data structures. Object-oriented languages such as C++ can handle a vast assortment of data structures, including custom classes and objects that reflect a specific real-life object or system of objects.

Records

A **record** is one of the simplest data structures. It contains one or more data elements and stores them in sequential positions in the computer's memory. In many cases, these elements are of completely different data types (e.g., integers, real numbers, strings, or any other type of value). A record consists of a name and different fields. Each field holds a data element. For example, a record might store information on a house. Each field within the record would contain a different characteristic of the house (e.g., square footage, dimensions, lot size, cost, street address, construction, names of owners, and any other pertinent information). Expressing these elements requires different data types, both numeric and textual. While records are a data structure in programming, they are also the building blocks of databases.

Integer Data Types

An **integer data type**, or **int**, contains a whole number. Using ints, programs can perform traditional arithmetic operations, such as addition and subtraction, and comparisons, such as less than, greater than, or equal to. In most cases, integer data is stored in **two's complement notation**, which allows efficient math on signed values (that is, values that are either positive or negative). Consider the following example:

```
int MaxOccupancy ← 300
```

This statement declares and initializes the variable: `int` specified a new variable of the integer data type, `MaxOccupancy` specifies the name of the variable, and `← 300` assigns the integer 300 as the value contained in the variable.

Real Data Types

Real data types are more often known simply as **floats** (short for "floating-point numbers") or **doubles** (referring to double-precision—the ability to store a wider range of floating-point numbers). These may contain numeric data other than whole numbers. They are stored in a floating-point notation. Real data types can be used in the same operations as integer data types, even though the actual methods of performing these operations will be different. Consider the following example:

```
float Length, Width, SquareFeet
Length ← 27.5
Width ← 18.4
SquareFeet ← Length * Width
```

In the above code, `float` declares a floating-point number variable, or real number variable. `Length`, `Width`, and `SquareFeet` are the names of the variables being declared. Often, multiple variables of the same data type can be declared in one statement. Two floating-point values are assigned to these variables, 27.5 to `Length`, and 18.4 to `Width`. `SquareFeet` is then assigned the value that the `*` operator will return when it multiplies the floats `Length` and `Width`. Even though the value will be a whole number, 506, it will actually be stored in memory as a float, because at least one of the two operands (`Length` and `Width`) was a float. It may not be obvious, but the operation called by the `*` operator in this case is different from the operation that the same operator would call if `Length` and `Width` were integers.

Character and Boolean Data Types

Character data types, often call **chars**, store combinations of numbers that map to actual characters (pieces of text). The system by which a program determines which character matches which numeric code is called **character encoding**. The most common encoding standard today is **Unicode**, while **ASCII** (American Standard Code for Information Interchange) remains familiar despite its limitation to Latin characters.

Chars can be used in the following operations, among others: comparing symbols to determine their correct alphabetical sequence; creating one long string of symbols by combining multiple, shorter strings of symbols; and determining the presence of one string of symbols inside another string. Below is a simple example of char declarations and assignments:

```
char Vowel, Consonant
Vowel ← 'a'
Consonant ← 't'
```

In the above example, `char` declares the variables, which are named `Vowel` and `Consonant`. Note that single quotes are used for the single characters assigned to the variables. In programming, often single quotation marks set off single characters, while double quotation marks set off strings (a different data type).

Boolean data types take their name from Boolean algebra, a system of logic defined by logician George Boole. Often referred to simply as **bools**, these data types can store only two values: true, represented in binary by a 1, or false, represented in binary by a 0. Therefore these data types require only one bit of storage. Many control structures and decision statements make use of bools, such as loops and if statements. Consider the following example:

```
bool hungry ← true
if(hungry)
   eat()
end if
```

In the above example, `bool` declares a Boolean variable named `hungry`, which is initialized with a value of `true`, or `1`. While if statements often use relational expressions that return a bool (for example, `x < 10`, which will return `true` or `1` when `x` is less than 10), they can also have a simple Boolean variable as their condition. In this case, `hungry` holds the value `true`, so the code block containing `eat()` will be executed.

Trees

A tree is a hierarchical abstract data structure that consists of **nodes**. The top node is known as the root node, while bottom nodes are known as terminal nodes or leaf nodes. Consider the following example:

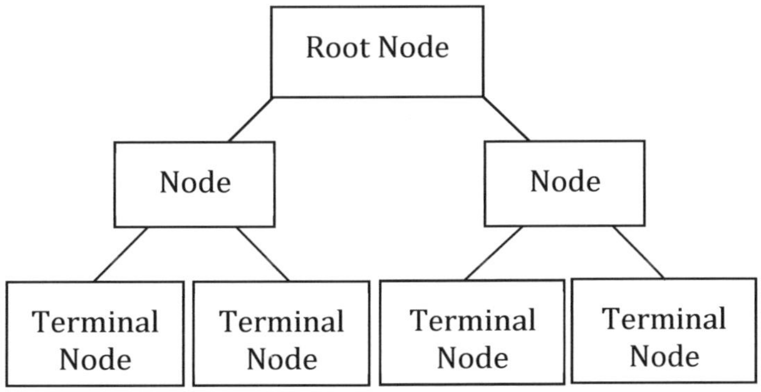

Nodes cannot be connected to more than one higher-level node. The depth of a **tree** is its total number of horizontal layers. In a binary tree, no node will have more than two descendants. A node's descendents are known as its "children." A node's ancestors nodes are known as its "parents." If we isolate one parent and its children, we have a subtree from the main tree.

STATIC VS. DYNAMIC ABSTRACT DATA STRUCTURES

Abstract data structures fall under two main categories:

- **Static structures** do not change in size or shape over time. Consider, for instance, a list of people born in a specific year. If the list is complete, it will neither increase nor decrease. The number will remain the same. Static structures are easier to maintain than dynamic structures because they only require a method of accessing data and changing data at a set location in memory, because no members need to be moved, removed, or added.
- **Dynamic structures** can change in size and shape over time. Consider a list of names of people who belong to a certain organization. As the organizaiton's membership increases or decreases, the list must change in size. Dynamic structures can be difficult to maintain because they require a method of adding or removing entries and acquiring more memory space if the structure grows.

IMPLEMENTATION STRATEGIES

FOR ONE-DIMENSIONAL HOMOGENOUS ARRAYS

One-dimensional homogenous arrays are ideal for storing sequences of data because they store data elements in consecutive memory cells. Consider the following example, which stores weekly weight measurements:

```
int[] Weight
```

The above declaration statement establishes a one-dimensional homogenous array referred to as `Weight`. It contains integer data types and consists of consecutive memory cells. If the address of the first entry in the array is `x`, the address of the other entries in the array can found easily because their position is sequential starting with `x`. For instance, the fifth entry in `Weight` would be located at the following address:

```
x + (5 - 1)
```

In other words, assuming that each member of the array occupies one memory address, a person could find the location of any array element by adding its zero-based index (hence the subtraction of 1) to the address of the beginning of the array.

FOR TWO-DIMENSIONAL HOMOGENOUS ARRAYS

Two-dimensional homogenous arrays are ideal for tables of information. They come in two varieties: **row-major order**, which stores data row by row in the computer's memory, and **column-major order**, which stores data column by column in the computer's memory. Consider the following example, a two-dimensional array that contains the weekly weight measurements of multiple people:

```
int[][] Weight
```

The above declaration statement establishes a two-dimensional homogenous array referred to as `Weight`. It contains int data types and consists of rows and columns. The entry in which the first row intersects the first column has the address of `x`. Assuming row-major order, a specific entry in the array could be located using the following formula:

```
x + (c * (i - 1)) + (j - 1)
```

In the above formula, `x` represents the address of the first element in the first column, `c` is the number of columns in the array, `i` is the row containing the desired entry, and `j` is the column containing the desired entry. The expression `(c * (i - 1))`, by multiplying the row index and the number of columns, "skips" the memory addresses for all the rows before the desired row. Then the expression `(j - 1)`, which will evaluate to the row index, adds the appropriate number of addresses.

For Heterogeneous Arrays

Consider the following fixed heterogeneous array, which contains the name of each product, its price, and the number sold:

```
struct Product {
char[] ProductName
float Price
    int UnitsSold
}
product[5]
```

The array consists of five sets of ten contiguous memory spaces. In each set, the first eight spaces contain character data types that identify the product's name. The ninth cell contains a float data type identifying the product's price. Finally, the tenth cell contains an integer data type identifying the number sold. Counting memory addresses here is more difficult than in homogeneous arrays, as each data type will occupy a different amount of memory. The char data type usually uses one byte, the float data type usually uses four, and the int data type usually uses four as well. Thus, each element of `Product` will use (8 * 1) + 4 + 4 = 16 bytes, and the entire array will therefore use 16 * 5 = 80 bytes.

To change the entry in `Price`, we would input the following statement:

```
product.Price ← 5.50
```

Note that we use a lowercase *p*, indicating that we are referring to the object `product`, which is an instance of the struct Product. In this example, the code is case-sensitive, and it is important to remember to use the instance of a class or type and not the class itself, unless it is defined as static. Using a lowercase first letter to indicate an instance of a class with the same name is a feature of the very common object-oriented programming language C++.

In non-managed languages, dynamic heterogeneous arrays are best created using pointers, which allow for memory management methods to be performed.

For Lists

A **contiguous list** is the best technique for storing static lists of names. It consists of a large block of memory cells, which are divided into groups to form subblocks. Each subblock stores a name on the list. For instance, 200 consecutive memory cells would be allocated for a contiguous list to accommodate 20 subblocks of 10 cells apiece. If a name on this list does not use the entire allotment of 10 cells, the empty cells are typically still filled, but with spaces.

A **linked list** is the best technique for storing dynamic lists. It relies on pointers, which enable each item on the list to point to the location of another item on the list, though the two items could be in very different locations in memory. This allows the data to be stored in various locations and linked together, instead of being stored on a large block of consecutive memory addresses. A program can therefore add information to the list without the risk of exceeding the capacity of a single, large block. Different languages handle the structure of linked lists differently, but a common set of characteristics includes each element in the list containing both a data field and a pointer field, where the pointer fields include pointers to the next (and sometimes also the previous) element. Linked lists may contain sentinel nodes, which demarcate the first and last elements in a list, or they could include null pointers to indicate that no node succeeds or precedes the current one.

For Stacks

When creating a stack, a programmer must allocate a memory block with sufficient space to hold the stack at its largest size. The first entry in the stack will form the base end. Additional entries are inserted by being stacked on top of the base entry. The top of the stack will change locations as the program pushes and pops entries; consequently, the address of the top must be marked by a **stack pointer**, which is stored in an additional memory cell. When a new entry is pushed onto the stack, the pointer will be pointing to the vacant location immediately above the most recently added entry. The new entry will be placed at this location. When an entry is popped out of the stack, the pointer will be pointing to the location immediately above the removed entry that is to be removed.

For Queues

When creating a queue, a programmer must allocate a memory block with sufficient space to hold the queue at its largest size. Information is pushed into the queue at the tail and popped out at the head. Consequently, there must be two pointers—a head pointer and a tail pointer—to track activity at both ends. The **tail pointer** always points to the first vacant location at the tail, and the **head pointer** always points to the first filled entry at the head. When the head and tail pointers are pointing at the same location, the queue is empty. In order to prevent the queue from crawling through the computer's memory, the programmer may implement a **circular queue**, which uses the vacated spaces at the head when adding an entry to the tail, thereby allowing the queue to loop through the same locations in memory.

For Binary Trees

In a binary tree, a parent node cannot have more than two child nodes. When stored in the computer's memory, binary trees usually rely on a linked structure with pointers. Each node counts as a single entry, and consists of three parts:

- Data contained in the node
- A **left child pointer** that points to the node's first child
- A **right child pointer** that points to the node's second child

The nodes at the bottom of the tree must use null pointers to indicate there are no additional nodes, and the node at the very top of the tree must be identified by **a root pointer**.

Binary trees are sometimes stored as a single block of contiguous memory cells in an ahnentafel list—a term and method borrowed from genealogy—rather than a linked structure. In such a list, the root node is followed by both its children—left then right—after which are the left child's two children and then the right child's two children. This pattern continues until the tree is finished. As one might notice, this is most efficient for complete trees.

Literals

A **literal** is a preset, unchanging value used by programs. Literals are set to a value directly instead of being assigned a variable. Consider, for instance, writing an error message in an application. The error message is triggered when a user attempts to enter text in a locked field. The developer might write a method for this error message as follows:

```
MessageBox("Entry is not allowed in field " + field1)
```

In this example, the literal is enclosed in quotation marks (the common method for denoting a string literal), and a variable is appended to the end. There would be no reason to assign the literal value to a variable, as the message will never need to be different, while the information that changes is derived from the value of `field1`.

Literals are problematic in programming for two reasons:

- They can be difficult to interpret and troubleshoot at a later date. This especially true of numeric values.
- They can be difficult to locate and alter in the program.

CONSTANTS

A **constant** is a name that describes an unchanging value. While variables provide a way to assign human-readable names to values that can be changed during the program, constants provide a way to assign human-readable names to values that will not change during the program. Constants remedy problems associated with literals, especially the difficulties of locating and changing literals. Consider the following declarative statements that establishes a constant:

```
const String c_companyName ← "Davis Company"
```

This statement assigns the name `c_companyName` to the value "Davis Company." Since the name of this company is not going to change while the program is running, to is helpful to have it readily accessible as a constant. In any place where the company name is needed, it is easy to include in a string of text:

```
String sGreeting ← "Welcome to "  + c_companyName + " !"
```

As the company's name is a constant value that is not expected to change at runtime, and it is likely to be referenced in many places, it makes sense to store it as a constant and place it in a global utility namespace for easy use throughout the program. This way, if the company were to change its name, a developer would only need to change the value of the constant `c_companyName`. Note that the main difference between a constant and a variable is that the constant, once initialized and assigned a value, cannot be changed by the program.

TYPE CONVERSION

Type conversion is the process of converting one data type to another. This is important mainly because of how computers store data. When a user enters information, it is common for programs to take it in as a string. However, if the information the user is entering is numerical data, there may be some need to do some calculations using this data, depending on the purpose of the program. Strings cannot be used in calculations the same way that integers and floats can. For example, if the string "6" is added to the string "4" using a plus sign, in most languages, the result will not be 10 but instead "64" because the plus operator will concatenate the two strings. If we want to add 6 and 4 mathematically, we must be working with values that are stored as numbers, not as text numerals. Since many inputs will be as text, but many calculations will need to be done using numbers, it is very helpful to have a built-in way to convert text to numbers and numbers to text. The same goes for conversion from an integer to a real number. If we try dividing 10 by 4 in code, since both numbers are integers, we will get 2 instead of 2.5. Dividing 10.0 by 4.0, on the other hand, will yield the answer that we understand as correct, 2.5. Because many built-in operations work differently when they are given different data types, the ability to convert one data type into another is an integral part of performing calculations correctly in programming.

Casting Between Data Types

Casting between data types is used when a programmer needs to either increase or decrease the functionality of an object. For example, in many programming languages, when you divide an integer value by another integer value, the answer will be returned as an integer. This often results in a loss of precision because a calculation such as 5 divided by 2 would yield a 2 rather than a 2.5 due to integer division. By casting one of the values, either the 5 or the 2, to a decimal before the calculation, we increase the functionality of the variable, allowing decimal division to be completed.

Code Examples

Example 1

Trace the following code and give the answer:

```
float ans ← (7 / 3) + (6 / 12.0) - (6 % 4)
```

This code will follow the rules of order of operations. First, `7 / 3` will occur. Because these numbers are both integers, integer division will occur, truncating any decimal values, leaving us with 2. Next, `6 / 12.0` will be performed, but as floating-point division, because at least one of the values is a floating-point number. This results in a value of 0.5. Lastly, `6 % 4` returns the remainder after dividing 6 by 4, which is 2. Therefore, we have 2 + 0.5 – 2, giving us 0.5 as the value of `ans`, which is a float data type, capable of storing a floating-point number.

Example 2

What numerical input for the integer variable x will result in the capital letter C being printed on the screen, assuming ASCII character codes?

```
char MyChar ← x
print x
```

When you declare and initialize a character variable, the data stored is a numerical code for a character, not the character itself. Characters are often declared using the character in single quotes, because the single quotes signal to the computer that the character should be stored as the corresponding numeric code. For example, the capital letter A would be represented as `'A'`. The most basic system for encoding characters is ASCII (American Standard Code for Information Interchange). In ASCII, each character of the Roman alphabet, each numeral, and several other characters each have a numeric code.

Therefore, when you declare a char variable and initialize it with a number value, like `x` in the above code, and notably not a letter in single quotes, the computer will interpret this number as a character code. Because the data type is char, the computer will simply represent the value as the corresponding letter, even though the value in memory is really a number. In ASCII, the capital letter *A* is 65. The other capital letters follow in alphabetical order; *B* is 66, *C* is 67, *D* is 68, and so on. Knowing this about ASCII, we will also know that "C" will be printed if the value of `x` is 67.

EXAMPLE 3

Write code to divide 13 by 5 and give the answer as a whole number and a remainder.

In order to get the whole number portion of a number as well as the remainder, we will need to perform two calculations on these numbers. First, we must use integer division to get the whole number. If you use the division operator with two variables of int data type, it will return only the whole number result and ignore any remainder. Next, we need to get the remainder that was ignored during the integer division. To do so, we must use the modulo operator. Rather than returning the whole number and ignoring the remainder, this operator returns the remainder and ignores the whole number. Once we have both these values, we can display each number individually.

```
int whole ← 13 / 5              //integer division
int remainder ← 13 % 5          //modulo division
print "The answer is " + whole + " with a remainder of " +
remainder
```

This will result in the following text being printed (assuming the `print` function or the plus operator will convert the integer values to text):

```
The answer is 2 with a remainder of 3
```

EXAMPLE 4

What is wrong with the statement below, and how could it be fixed?

```
int total ← 4.7 * 2
```

In this example, `4.7 * 2` will give the answer 9.2. Since this is a floating-point number, we are unable to store it directly in the `total` variable, because it is defined as an integer. In many languages, this statement would not compile, because compilers themselves are written to assume we want an integer to be stored in variables of the integer data type. The only way we can store this value is by adding some type of operation to convert the result of the multiplication into an integer. We can do this in a few ways. We could simply truncate the number by removing the decimal point and the digit after it. We could also use a math function to round down to 9. Still another option would be to use a type conversion function to convert the answer to an integer before storing it in the variable `total`. Programming languages and development environments will vary in how they interpret a statement like the one above, how they alert the developer to this issue, and what built-in functions they provide to allow the developer to fix the problem.

EXAMPLE 5

Write an equivalent statement using a loop to simulate the modulo operator.

In module division, we can forget entirely about the actual quotient—or number of times that the divisor "goes into" the dividend. We only need to find the remainder, and it is not overly complicated to develop a loop that does this. One possibility is the following:

```
int modulo(int dividend, int divisor)
   while(dividend > divisor)
```

```
        dividend ← dividend - divisor
    end while
    return dividend
end modulo
```

This code uses repeated subtraction to continually reduce the dividend by the divisor. Once `dividend` is no longer greater than `divisor`, we know that the divisor cannot "go into" `dividend` one whole time, so the new value of `dividend` must be the remainder. This is the value that the function returns.

Integer vs. Floating-Point Data Types

An integer is a data type that can only store a number that does not contain a decimal point. The number can be negative or zero, but it cannot contain a fraction, a decimal point, or any digits to the right of the decimal point. Examples of integers are −45, 0, and 32. You might use an integer to give someone's age in years, or to count how many items you have purchased from a store. A floating-point number, or float, is a data type that stores numbers with a decimal point and up to a certain number of significant digits. Examples of floating-point numbers are 4.0, −20.45, 0.0, and 3.14159. You might use a floating-point number to calculate a grade point average or when doing calculations with numbers that contain fractional values, such as pi. Many students ask why we can't just use a floating-point number for everything, since it can store whole numbers as well as numbers with fractions. The answer is that floating-point numbers usually take up more space in memory and are harder for the computer to calculate with. In fact, when you store a whole number as a float, the number that is stored is of the same precision as any other float; in other words, the whole number 3 would be stored not as 3 but as 3.000000. Therefore, when possible, we use the integer data type when we do not need the precision of a float.

Efficiency of Using Boolean Data Type vs. Using a String

The first advantage of using a Boolean data type instead of a string data type for a value that can be "yes" or "no" is that Booleans take up minimal space in memory. Because a Boolean variable can contain only two possible values, it needs only one bit of memory—though in many languages, the minimum allocation for any variable is one byte. A string can be much larger, and storing the actual text "yes", "no", "true", or "false" would certainly take more than one byte. The exact difference between the space used by the two types will depend on the programming language being used, but generally, a Boolean takes up less space.

The second advantage of using a Boolean data type is that, when they are used in if statements, since there are only two possibilities, an else statement can be readily used, rather than testing for other cases. For example:

```
if(raining == true)
    print "Bring an umbrella."
else
    print "Don't bring an umbrella."
end if
```

Because the above Boolean `raining` has only two possible values, we only have to check if it is true, and we can use an else statement to handle the only other case—that `raining` is false. If we had instead used a string in this situation, we would have to check if `raining` contained "yes", then check if `raining` contained "no", and finally add an else statement to check for any other possibility that wasn't expected.

CODE EXAMPLE

Imagine a program to run a vending machine that only accepts bills (no coins), contains items that can be any price, and gives the appropriate amount of change for each transaction. This particular vending machine contains only peanuts and cashews. Identify the variable types that would be best to use for the number of bills, the item price, the type of item, and the change.

The variable for the number of bills should be an integer because the machine only accepts bills and no decimal point is needed when counting whole bills. The variable for the prices of the items should be a floating-point number, because the prices could be any dollar amount, not only whole dollars. A variable for item type could be a string for a typical vending machine. But in this case, it would be more efficient to use a Boolean, as there are only two items available. If the vending machine had the ability to hold more than two items, a data type with more than two possible values would be necessary. Lastly, the change that is given should be a floating-point number, because, like the prices of the items, the change for a transaction may not be a whole dollar amount.

CONCATENATION

Concatenation is the process of combining two strings together to form a new string. The most common concatenation operator is the plus symbol, but it can vary from one programming language to another.

CODE EXAMPLE

A program stores the first name "John" in `fName`*, the last name "Kennedy" in* `lName`*, and the middle initial "F" in* `mInitial`*. Write code to concatenate these variables so that a string named* `fullName` *contains the string "Kennedy, John F."*

The solution to this question lies in ordering our variables correctly (so that the last name is first), along with adding the necessary spaces, the comma after the last name, and the period after the middle initial.

```
String fullName ← lName + ", " + fName + " " + mInitial + "."
```

This code would result in the correct concatenation being stored in `fullName`. Notice the use of the literal space and comma characters. Without including those, the pieces of the text would be mashed together, resulting in an incorrect format. These characters must also be enclosed in double quotes to denote that they are literal strings. The variable names must not have quotes around them, because the values of the variables are needed. If they had quotes around them, the concatenation operators would interpret them as literal strings, so the names of the variables would be the text used; the result would be "lName, fName mInitial."

Writing and Calling Procedures

PROCEDURES

A **procedure** is a set of instructions that carry out a certain function. By including all the steps of a function in a single procedure, developers are able repeat common tasks with a single call of this procedure, rather than needing to enter the steps again and again. Furthermore, if a task needs to be done differently, and that task has an associated procedure, the change need only be made in one place, rather than in every part of the code that performs the task. For instance, if a program needed to set a piece of data in a database, the developer could write code that connects to the database each time the data is to be set, sets the data, and closes the connection. What if the databases's name or connection information changed? Without a procedure, the developer would have to find all the places where the program code accesses the database—which could be hundreds or thousands of places. Because this would be impracticable, a procedure that sets the data would likely be made, and this procedure could be called whenever a piece of data is to be set. Then the developer would be able to make any necessary changes only once, in this procedure, saving countless hours of time and potentially many errors.

A procedure always has a name, which is written in the code when the procedure is called. This name is set when the procedure is defined. A procedure can be written to accept certain data that it will need to perform its function; these are called **parameters**. The actual values that are passed to the procedure through these parameters are called **arguments**. Procedures give control back to the main part of the program when they return a value.

If data is needed from the procedure, the type of data is often used to define the procedure. For example, a procedure that finds the lowest integer in a list would likely return the integer, so it might be defined `int GetLowest(list[])`. This data is returned to the main part of the program when the procedure ends.

On the other hand, if (as in our original database example), no data is needed from the procedure, it can be written to return a value such as zero to signifying that it ran successfully. The declaring statement for such a procedure might be `void SetData(FieldName, FieldData)`, with "void" meaning that no value will be returned.

See the following pseudocode of our database example:

```
/* open() and close() are procedures that connect to and
disconnect from (respectively) a given database */

void SetData(FieldName, FieldData)
   open(database1)
   FieldName ← FieldData
   close(database1)
end SetData
```

In this example, `SetData` is the procedure's name, and `FieldName` and `FieldData` are parameters, which allowing any data to be passed to the procedure. Anywhere in the code, a developer could set the CustomerCount field in the database to the integer 15,000 by writing the following:

```
SetData(CustomerCount, 15000)
```

If the information needed to connect to the database should ever change, now only `SetData` needs to be modified.

Code Example

A method named `getLowest` *accepts a list of integers as well as the number of integers in that list and returns the lowest number in the list. Write the method, and then code to use this method to find the lowest number in each of the three lists below. Display the sum of those numbers and store it in a variable named* `sum`.
List 1: 3, 6, 5

List 2: 4, 1
List 3: 5, 4, 9, 6

The method can use a variable called `lowest` to hold the lowest value in the list. First, the method sets the first value in the list as `lowest`. Then, a for loop will step through each value of the list. Finally, an if statement inside the for loop can reassign the current value as `lowest` if it is less than the value already contained in `lowest`. This method could be written as follows:

```
int getLowest(int[] list, int size)
   int lowest ← list[0]
   for(int i ← 0; i < size; i ← i + 1)
      if(list[i] < lowest)
         lowest ← list[i]
      end if
   end for
end getLowest
```

Once the method is written, calling the method for each of the three lists and storing the summed result in an int variable is straightforward:

```
int sum ← getLowest(list1, 3) + getLowest(list2, 2) +
   getLowest(list3, 4)
```

Creating User-Defined Functions

The exact process and syntax for creating a user-defined function varies among programming languages. However, the high-level process is generally the same. First, the developer must create a name for the function. Keywords of the language cannot be used, nor can the names of any predefined functions. In most cases, the name must start with a letter and can only contain letters and numbers. In most languages, the developer will also need to determine what the data type of the output will be, because this information will be part of the function declaration statement. Next, the developer must specify the number and types of inputs that need to be provided to the function. For example, does the function need a single string as an input, or does it require four integers? After the inputs have been specified, the developer will write the function code. This is where the work is performed and the inputs are used to produce an output. The final step is generally to return the output to the main function. Some languages include a "success" value that can be returned by functions that do not have an output, while others may allow functions to simply end, and still others may specify that an otherwise normal value will signify success when it is returned by a function.

Reasons for Creating User-Defined Functions

Typically, a developer creates a user-defined function because the functionality that is needed is not included in a predefined function of the language. In many cases, a developer does this when they also see a need to reuse the custom functionality over and over again. It is generally not worth the extra effort to create a user-defined function if the functionality is only needed once. In that case, the developer only needs to create the functionality once in the main program. However, it is more often the case that a program needs some procedure to be performed multiple times. It is these cases where user-defined functions are very useful. The developer also has strict control over the inputs and outputs of any user-defined functions they create.

Using and Calling User-Defined Functions

User-defined functions are generally called in the same way that predefined functions are called. The specific syntax required varies from language to language, but the calling of the function is done using the name of the function along with the inputs. The function itself specifies the number and types of inputs that should be provided. Once the function is called, then control over the processing is passed from the main program to the function. The function performs its specified action, and then passes the result and processing control back over to the main program. The same function may be called multiple times in the same main program.

Return

The term "return" refers to the manner in which outputs are provided from a function back to the main program. The word "return" is used because the function takes an input from the main program, performs work on the input, and then returns with the data back to the main program. With user-defined functions, the developer has complete control over the number and types of outputs that are returned. In addition to user-defined functions, predefined functions also return outputs to the main program. However, in these cases, the developer does not have control over the number or types of outputs that are returned. The predefined function must be used as is, and the returned outputs should be handled appropriately.

Arguments

An argument is a value that is passed between programs, routines, or functions. In many cases, this argument is a variable that is used to store a value. When a user-defined function is created, the developer specifies the types and number of inputs that will be provided to the function. These inputs are called "parameters." Upon calling the function in the main program, the developer must specify the values that will be passed to the function in these parameters. These values are the arguments. As an example, consider a function `mult(a, b)` that requires parameters `a` and `b` to be numbers. When the function is called in code using the numbers 3 and 4 as inputs, the statement will be written `mult(3, 4)`. In this scenario, 3 and 4 are the arguments. Interestingly, not all functions require arguments to be passed to them. A function can be written to operate without any inputs, and such a function can still return an output value.

Parameters

The terms "parameter" and "argument" are sometimes used interchangeably, although there is a distinct difference between the two. Remember that an argument is an actual value passed to a function or subroutine. A parameter, however, is the item that specifies what type of value needs to be passed. A parameter is used in the definition and creation of the function to specify what type of input the function requires. For example, if a function is defined as `mult(a, b)`, then `a` and `b` are the parameters of the function. When the function is called in the main program as `mult(1, 2)`, then 1 and 2 are the arguments being passed.

Passing an Argument by Value vs. Passing by Reference

When parameters are passed to a function, they can be passed either by value or by reference. Passing by value is straightforward. The value itself is passed to the function. This could be an integer value, like 2, or a character, like "a" or another letter. Passing by reference is more complicated. When a reference is passed to a function, instead of passing the value itself to the function, the value's location in memory is passed. This may be done using a pointer or using a variable that is of a reference data type, such as a string. When the function needs to manipulate that value, it uses the reference to find the value located at that memory address. Remember the difference between primitive and reference data types. Reference data types are automatically passed by reference when they are used as an input to a function. This can be useful when the developer needs to make changes to a value that is passed in as an argument, but for one reason or another cannot easily return the value at the end of the function.

Propagated Arguments Passed by Reference

In some cases, it may be necessary for changes made to inputs of a function to be propagated throughout the entire program, even though those changes may not necessarily be considered formal outputs. In this case, it is necessary to pass these inputs into the function by reference. When arguments are passed by reference, the address of the value in memory is passed instead of the value itself. When the value of the argument is changed, the value stored at that memory location gets updated to reflect the new value. Later in the program, when that memory address is accessed, the new value will used because that is the value currently stored at that location. This is how a developer can propagate changes to an argument throughout an entire program. It should be noted that some modern programming languages do not support true passing by reference, but in such languages there is generally a way of accomplishing the same result.

Deciding to Pass a Parameter by Value or by Reference

The main factor that will affect this decision is whether the function or subroutine should be able to make changes to the inputs that will be visible throughout the rest of the program. If not, then the arguments should be passed by value. In effect, this creates a duplicate, independent variable within the function that is only editable within the function, and indeed only exists while the function is running. Whatever variable was passed to the function from the main program does not undergo any changes. If these variables need to be changed in the main program, then they should be passed to the function by reference. This way, the main program and the function are both effectively using the same variable. Inside the function, the variable is handled like any other variable would be, but the changes made to it are being automatically applied to the value that the main-program variable is assigned to.

Parameters That Are Automatically Passed by Reference

Some data types are automatically passed by reference due to the way they are stored in memory. Remember that primitive data types are small pieces of data that can generally be stored completely within the register of the CPU. These types of parameters can be passed by value. However, some data types are stored in other areas of memory and are referred to with a memory address. Some examples of these data types include lists, strings, and arrays. Since these are referenced by a call to a memory location, these types of parameters are automatically passed by reference and not by value.

Passing Arrays to Functions

Arrays are passed to functions by reference. This means that the array in the main program that is passed to the function is effectively being used inside the function as well—any changes made to it are going to be made to the location in memory that the entire program is referencing. The actual data that is passed from the main program into the function is the memory address of the first item in the array. This is often called the **first address** or **foundation address**. With the first address as a point of reference, the function can access the space in memory where the array is stored. In accordance with how arrays are stored in memory, since all the items in the array are the same type and size, the function can access any element in the array.

Efficiency in Storing Arrays

It is generally a good idea to store all arrays in a program using the same method. This makes things less confusing because a consistent method is followed. If some arrays are stored in row-major order while others are in column-major order, a developer will be more likely to inadvertently access an incorrect array element. However, in some cases, it can be more efficient to store some arrays in row-major order and others in column-major order. This typically occurs when operations are being performed that require specific handling of both arrays at once. Matrix multiplication is a great example of this. When matrix multiplication is performed, the program can step through each row of one matrix while stepping through each column of the other. This makes matrix multiplication much more efficient than having both arrays stored in the same manner.

Common Input Methods

There are many ways that inputs are taken into a system. The most rudimentary is for input values to be hard coded into the program itself. Such a program is not scalable, as there is no way to for someone using the program to change the inputs. This is typically only done by those who are learning to program or developers trying to make an algorithm.

A far more common way to provide input is with prompts or fields that accept inputs typed on a keyboard. Another common form of input is through buttons or other controls that can be clicked on using a mouse or touchscreen. In addition to keyboards and mice, existing files may also be used as input to a program. A user can put all necessary data in the file with a certain format that the program is designed to read, and the program can then read the file and use or manipulate the information contained in the file.

Common Ways to Handle Output

At some point, the output from most programs needs to be in a format that is consumable by a human being. There are several ways of accomplishing this. The most common way to handle output in the early days of personal computers was through text displayed on a screen. Since then, **graphical user interfaces** (GUIs) have become virtually ubiquitous. In these cases, outputs may be given to the user through anything that can be put on a screen, including not only text in a console but also images, videos, and digital visualizations of documents. Another way to handle output is through printed materials. The program may print items onto a physical medium like paper so that a human is able to read the output in a physical form.

Functions

In some programming languages, a **function** and a **procedure** are the same thing, and they may also be called routines, subroutines, or methods. However, in some programming languages, a function is different from a procedure. In these cases, a procedure is a set of steps that perform some kind of task. A function, on the other hand, is a procedure that returns a value to the calling code. Consider the following example:

```
float SquareFootage(float Length, float Width)
   float SquareFeet
   SquareFeet ← Length * Width
   return SquareFeet
end SquareFootage
```

The first line is the function's header, which declares the data type that will be returned (in this case a float), the name of the function (`SquareFootage`), and the formal parameters. Inside the function, a local variable named `SquareFeet` is declared, `SquareFeet` is given the value of the `Length` and `Width` variables multiplied together, and finally `SquareFeet` is returned to the calling code. This function could be called in the main program or parent function as follows:

```
float Price ← 100 * SquareFootage(100, 200)
```

The above statement calls the `SquareFootage` function and assigns actual parameters 100 and 200 to the formal parameters. The returned float is multiplied by 100, and the result becomes the value of the float variable `Price`.

Methods

While the term "method" can be used broadly to refer to a set of steps (i.e., a procedure) or a particular process for solving a problem (i.e., an algorithm), it has a more specific meaning in object-oriented programming. In object-oriented languages, a **method** is a procedure or function that is a member of an object. Methods help to determine how their parent object will respond to a wide range of events. In the object-oriented paradigm, every system consists of objects. Each object performs a specific set of functions and interacts with other objects to solve problems. Consider, for instance, an object-oriented program that makes uses of spreadsheets. A particular spreadsheet might be an object, and it may have one method to open it, one to save it, one to insert rows, one to insert columns, and so on. In the common programming language C++, methods are often known as **member functions**.

IDEs and Programming Language Paradigms

Visual Development Environments

A **visual development environment** (**VDE**) enables a computer programmer to use the shortcut of point-and-click technology instead of laboriously typing out all the code. Sometimes, computer programs contain repetitions of vast code strings which can be extremely tedious to retype; a VDE eliminates that tedium. Often, a VDE also contains a form design grid with which the programmer can design the user interface. Most VDEs also allow customization by the user. For instance, a programmer may be able to choose from a background color for a program.

Integrated Development Environments (IDEs)

Characteristics of an IDE

An **integrated development environment** (**IDE**) is a single environment available to a programmer that has many development tools integrated into one. The use of an IDE means the developer does not need to have a separate tool for each of the many common tasks associated with developing a program, including coding, compiling, debugging, and testing. It also helps to cut down on development time because, again, the developer does not have to perform these tasks separately. They can all be performed inside of the IDE as development occurs. Visual Studio is a very common and widely used IDE. Most developers are familiar with this IDE, even if they do not use it on an everyday basis.

Components Included in an IDE

Different integrated development environments (IDEs) contain different components. However, there are some components that are generally common to all IDEs. These components include **source code editors** and **debuggers**. Many IDEs also contain a **compiler**. Some other components that might be offered in an IDE include an interpreter, an auto-complete editor, and version control. More recent IDEs usually contain tools for use in object-oriented programming, such as class browsers and object browsers. An IDE may be built with a certain language in mind, and which IDE is most commonly used by developers varies from language to language. Individual developers may also have their own preferences regarding which IDE to use or whether to use an IDE at all. The best-known IDE today is Visual Studio.

Effect on Development Times

An IDE can shorten development times primarily due their integration of the various tools that are needed and their user-friendliness. An IDE contains the main tools that a developer needs, and these tools are already integrated. There is no need for the developer to use separate compilers, debuggers, or other tools to complete the development work. Not having to integrate these separate tools can save a great deal of time. Modern IDEs are also relatively user friendly. They often have features that save typing time and help to avoid simple mistakes. For example, an IDE might feature automatically completed typing of commands, functions, or variables. It may also color-code items so that the developer not only knows that they have typed the item correctly, but they also know how the compiler will interpret that item. For example, built-in functions may be in blue text, while user-defined functions are in green text, and variables are in orange text. The IDE might also have a variable viewer, which will allow the developer to step through lines of code and see how the values of individual variables change with the execution of each line. Compared to typing raw code into a text file, coding with these user-friendly features takes far less time and effort.

Advantages

There are several advantages to using an IDE. The most obvious is that it makes development work easier for the developer. Many IDEs include features like intuitive code editors and visual tools, which make coding faster and more convenient. Furthermore, IDEs reduce development times because separate tools are not necessary, which makes the process of coding, compiling, and debugging less complex and time-consuming. Finally, IDEs are very helpful for debugging, because they generally include step-based debugging tools that show the developer what happens for each line of code.

Programming Paradigms

Object-Oriented Paradigm

The object-oriented paradigm views software systems as collections of objects. It led to the emergence of object-oriented programming, or OOP. Each object in a program consists of data and a set of procedures (known as methods) for interacting with that data. Objects can work with other objects in order to solve problems and generate certain outcomes. Consider, for instance, a text document that contains sales data. Under the **object-oriented paradigm**, the document is created as an object containing information (i.e., sales data) and methods for changing that data (i.e., adding data, deleting data, sorting, etc.). Assume the program wants to extrapolate sales projections. By having the sales data object interact with an object containing mathematical functions, the program could generate the desired projections. There are a few key terms associated with the object-oriented paradigm:

- An **object** is a programming unit consisting of data and methods for interacting with that data.
- A **class** acts like a template for objects. Multiple objects may be based on the same lines of written code. All objects based on this code are the same class.
- An **instance** is an "instance of a class"—or in other words, a specific object.

Imperative Paradigm

The **imperative paradigm**, or **procedural paradigm**, views programs as sequences of commands that control data and perform calculations in order to "solve" a particular program. This paradigm aligns well with what people generally view computer programming to be. It serves as the basis for machine language and pseudocode. The programmer develops an algorithm that tells the computer what to do, and this sequence of commands carries out the algorithm, performing an operation or generating an output.

Declarative Paradigm

The **declarative paradigm** views programs as descriptions of data and the logical relationshps governing it. The programmer provides a description of the problem to the programming system, and the system solves the problem using a series of general-purpose, problem-solving algorithms. Consequently, the focus is on creating the logical relationships that represent the system or problem rather than on writing algorithms. Logical programming languages are a very common type of declarative language. Declarative programming finds more uses in artificial intelligence, natural language processing, and higher-level mathematics than it does in traditional development of information systems.

Functional Paradigm

The **functional paradigm** views programming in terms of a mathematical function with an input-to-output relationship. In essence, the program is series of functions that accept input and generate output. The output of one function becomes input for another function, and so on. In this way, predefined functions (also known as predefined programming units) can be nested inside one another with simpler functions going inside the more complex functions.

Basic Steps Associated with Software Development

There are some basic steps that are common to computer program design, regardless of which design methodology a developer or team may be following. The first step is to determine the requirements for the software. The developer must know, in relatively exact terms, what the software needs to do. The next basic step is to design the solution, typically through the creation of an algorithm. After this, the actual coding can be done. After coding is completed, then testing must be performed to ensure that the software functions as anticipated. The type and length of testing is often determined by the specific model being followed. After testing is completed, the software can be released, and it then enters the maintenance phase. It can remain in the maintenance phase for years in some cases.

Categories of Program Statements

Statements that make up a procedural or object-oriented program generally fall under three categories:

- **Declarative statements** define the terminology that is unique to the program so that the terms may be used later in the program. Common examples of items that are declared in statements are variables, functions, constants, and classes.
- **Imperative statements**, also called **expressions**, are the instructions that tell the computer which operations or computations to do for each step of an algorithm.
- **Control flow statements** dictate which statements will be executed. Some control flow statements, such as if statements, may specify that a statement or block of statements will only execute if a given condition is true. Other control flow statements, such as for loops, may specify that a statement or block of statements be executed a given number of times.

Most programs follow the same basic structure, which starts with declarative statements and then has a main body of control flow statements and imperative statements. Other functions may be declared in the initial portion, but they are normally written after or below the main function.

Name Binding

Name binding is the process of associating a programming object, such as data or code, with an identifier. Programming languages perform name binding as an aid to programmers. Once an identifier is associated with an object, the identifier is described as "referencing" that object. Binding is related to scope, because scope dictates which objects are referenced by which identifiers, both in the human-readable code and when the code is executed. If binding occurs before the program runs, it is described as **static name binding**. If binding occurs while the program is running, it is described as **dynamic name binding**. In dynamic binding, the program receives both the request for the object and the object itself at runtime. Dynamic dispatch is a type of dynamic name binding used by several languages, including C++.

Concurrent Processing

Concurrent processing is the ability of a program or operating system to keep a number of processes logically active concurrently even though only one operation can take place at a time. The operating system creates this illusion of **concurrently active processes** by interleaving the execution order of their commands, thus juggling the execution of many processes at once. Problems may arise when the processes must communicate between themselves or access the same resources.

Issue of Communication

In concurrent processing, a main program simultaneously opens and operates multiple other programs. In many cases, one program may need to reach a certain point before another can continue running; consequently, they must communicate between themselves as they execute. Consider, for instance, two programs that must update a list. If they access the list at the same time, it may result in only one update being applied and the other update being lost. To avoid this problem, programmers must design the system such that certain data items are given **mutually exclusive access**, meaning only one application can access them at any given time. There are two methods for achieving mutually exclusive access:

- Program each application so that it can identify all the other applications and block their access when it is accessing the data. This method can be problematic because the whole system can crash from an error in one segment.
- Program the data item itself with a **monitor**, which prevents other applications from accessing it when it is already being accessed.

Event-Driven Programming

Event-driven programming allows the tasks in a program to vary based on some input provided to the system. This input could come from the system itself, another system, or a human user. Event-driven programming uses **event handlers**. The program "listens" for events and stores information about each event as it happens. When there is an event, and event handler determines what action needs to be taken based on the specifics of the event. Event-driven programming can become very complex, as some systems have a very large number of events that could occur. It is necessary to account for all these events so that the program knows how to react when any one of them occurs.

Synchronous and Asynchronous Sequential Systems

Synchronous sequential systems use digital circuits that are synchronized by clock signals, which are governed by a specific timing margin. When a clock signal is sent, the entire system changes state. A sequential system consists of a combinational logic device and a state register. When the state changes, the state register sends the previous combinational logic state as an input through the combinational logic device. The clock should only move as quickly as required to calculate the most time-intensive calculation.

Asynchronous sequential systems are not governed by clocks; rather, they have modular designs consisting of numerous concurrent hardware devices that achieve synchronization through communication interfaces. Asynchronous systems are typically more difficult to design because they must account for all possible states in all possible timings. If they fail to do so, the logic will be unstable. However, stable asynchronous systems are considered superior to synchronous systems because they run as fast as their gates allow.

Parallel Processing

Parallel processing occurs when a computer performs several tasks or actions simultaneously. It requires multiple processing units and has given rise to multiprocessor machines. There are two common number of architectures for parallel processing:

- **MIMD**, or **multiple instruction, multiple data**, involves connecting multiple processing units (i.e., CPUs) to the same main memory. This way, each processor can function independently while synchronizing its work with other processors by leaving messages in common memory cells. This architecture allows different instruction sets to be performed on different data sets.
- **SIMD**, or **single instruction, multiple data**, involves linking several processors together so they can simultaneously execute the same instruction on different sets of data. This architecture is best suited for situations where the same tasks must be performed on a large block of data.

Accessibility Features

Although people generally use mice, keyboards, monitors, and headphones or speakers to interact with computers, there are also many people with disabilities that restrict or prevent their use of one or more of these devices. Such people make up one of the major groups affected by the digital divide—the gap between people who use computers and the internet and people who do not. Bringing accessibility features to these people helps to bridge the digital divide.

Some examples of accessibility features are text-to-speech, speech-to-text, high-contrast display modes, head/mouth stick keyboards, increased font size, increased window size, keyboard access to all features, and tooltips or alt text. When writing programs, these accessibility options should be incorporated into the user interface, so that the effect of disabilities on user experience is minimized.

Periodically Updating Software

There are several reasons why software must be periodically updated. One of the most obvious reasons is to correct bugs or defects. The longer a piece of software is used and the more people it is used by, the more likely it is that bugs or other issues will be found that were not noticed before the initial release of the software. Updates are needed to correct such issues. Another reason for periodic updates is to handle new user requirements. As technologies advance, users generally expect their software to advance as well. Fulfilling new user requirements usually involves adding new features and functionality. One more major reason why software may need to be updated is to maintain compatibility with operating systems or other platforms. Operating systems themselves often undergo updates, and some updates may cause support for older pieces of software to cease. Therefore, these older pieces of software require updates in order to remain available to users.

NEGATIVE IMPACTS OF NOT UPDATING

A lack of updates to a piece of software can have many negative consequences. One of the most catastrophic consequences could be that the software ceases to function at all. Other challenging but less devastating effects include the necessity to implement workarounds. This occurs when a defect is discovered, but no fix is implemented. Users must find a way to work around the defect. This is not ideal because it typically leads to increased work effort and decreased overall efficiency. Lastly, a lack of updates leads to an increased cost of ownership for a piece of software.

INCREASED COST OF OWNERSHIP DUE TO LACK OF UPDATES

Software that is not updated on a regular basis becomes more and more costly to own. One reason for this is because defects are not corrected. As defects arise, users must find other ways to work around these defects. This leads to the process taking more time to complete, which results in lost productivity. Additionally, when there are no updates to software, features that become necessary are never added to the software. Thus the needed functionality must be obtained elsewhere, often through the purchase of an additional piece of software. Furthermore, as a given copy of software gets older, it may become less efficient and require more hardware or system resources, it may become susceptible to costly malware or other attacks as vulnerabilities are found, and it may become incompatible with operating systems or other software that is integrated with it, requiring the use of virtual machines or other workarounds. At some point in time, the software becomes so costly that continuing to use the software is not feasible.

Chapter Quiz

Ready to see how well you retained what you just read? Scan the QR code to go directly to the chapter quiz interface for this study guide. If you're using a computer, simply visit the online resources page at **mometrix.com/resources719/texescompsci241** and click the Chapter Quizzes link.

Specialized Topics

Discrete Mathematics in Computer Science

Discrete Mathematics

Among mathematicians, there is not an agreed-upon definition of discrete math. What is agreed upon is the fact that discrete math deals with processes that use a finite, or countable, number of elements. In discrete math, the elements will be discontinuous, as this branch of mathematics does not involve the continuity that processes of calculus do. Generally, discrete math uses countable sets of rational numbers, although they do not use the set of all real numbers, as that would then make the math continuous and put it in the category of algebra or calculus. Discrete math has numerous applications in the fields of computer science and business.

Element of a Set

A **set** is a mathematical collection of items, and an **element** is an item that is included in the set. These items are typically sets of numbers, or sets of geometrical points, or even sets of sets.

Whether an item is an element of a set is a binary property. In other words, a particular item either is or is not an element of a given set. There are not different degrees of belonging to a set, and one element of a set cannot be more an element than another. Additionally, the elements do not have any particular order, and there is no count of how many times an element appears in a set. For example, in the set $\{0, 2, 1, 2, 4\}$, the numbers 0, 1, 2, and 4 are elements of the set. Two is not more of an element than the others because it is listed twice. Any number other than these, such as 3, is not an element of the set.

The mathematical symbol $\in$ means "is an element of." for instance, "$1 \in A$" means that "the number 1 is an element of set A". The symbol can be negated with a diagonal slash, so "$1 \notin A$" means "the number 1 is NOT an element of set A."

Empty Set

The **empty set** contains no elements. The symbol for the empty set is a circle with a line through it, $\emptyset$, or the empty set can be written in roster form as $\{\quad\}$. Although it may seem trivial, the empty set is important for the same reason that zero is an important number: without the empty set, many set operations and definitions would be incomplete. For instance, the intersection of two non-overlapping sets is the empty set. The set of all prime numbers that are perfect squares is the empty set, because there are no such numbers. Other sets can be constructed using the empty set. For instance, a set *containing* the empty set, $\{\{\quad\}\}$ or $\{\emptyset\}$, is different from the empty set itself, since it's not actually empty—it contains one element, the empty set.

The empty set is, by definition, a subset of every set, including itself. This is because every element that is an element of the empty set is also an element of any other set, since the empty set contains no elements that could make this statement false.

Subset, Proper Subset, and Superset

Set A is a **subset** of set B if set A is contained entirely within set B. More formally, set A is a subset of set B if every element of set A is also in set B. We can write this as $\forall x(x \in A \Rightarrow x \in B)$. The symbol for subset is $\subseteq$, so we can write "$A \subseteq B$" to mean "set A is a subset of set B," or "$A \nsubseteq B$" to mean "set A is NOT a subset of set B".

Any set is a subset of itself, since naturally any element in a set is in that set. A **proper subset** means a subset that is not equal to the other set. In other words, set A is a proper subset of set B if set A is a subset of set B but they are not the same, so $A \subseteq B$ but $B \nsubseteq A$. For example, $\{0,1,2\}$ is a proper subset of $\{0,1,2,3\}$ because every element in the first set is included in the second set, but the two sets are not identical. The symbol for a proper subset is $\subset$, so we write "$A \subset B$" to mean "set A is a proper subset of set B," and "$A \not\subset B$" to mean "set A is NOT a proper subset of set B."

The converse of a subset is a **superset**. If A is a subset of B, then B is a superset of A. In the example above, $\{0,1,2,3\}$ is a superset of $\{0,1,2\}$ because the first set contains every element of the second plus more.

Union of Two or More Sets

The **union** of two or more sets includes all the elements that are included in all of the sets. An element is in the union of sets A and B if it is in set A or in set B, or if it is in both. The union is written with the symbol $\cup$, so "$A \cup B$" (read "A union B") means the union of sets A and B.

For example, given the sets $A = \{1,2,3,4\}$ and $B = \{2,4,6,8\}$, then $A \cup B = \{1,2,3,4,6,8\}$. 1 and 3 are in $A \cup B$ because they are in set A, and 6 and 8 are in $A \cup B$ because they are in set B. 2 and 4 appear in both A and B, so they are in $A \cup B$, but they only appear once.

The union operation on sets is both commutative and associative. That is, $A \cup B = B \cup A$, and $(A \cup B) \cup C = A \cup (B \cup C)$.

Intersection of Two or More Sets

The intersection of two or more sets is a set including every element that appears in *all* of the sets. An element is in the intersection of sets A and B if and only if the element appears in both set A and set B. For instance, if set $A = \{0,1,2,3\}$ and set $B = \{2,3,4,5\}$, the intersection of sets A and B includes the elements 2 and 3, because these are the only elements that appear in both sets. The intersection is written with the symbol $\cap$, so "$A \cap B$" (read "A intersection B") means the intersection of sets A and B.

The intersection operation on sets is both commutative and associative. That is, $A \cap B = B \cap A$, and $(A \cap B) \cap C = A \cap (B \cap C)$. The union and intersection operations also jointly have distributive properties: $A \cap (B \cup C) = (A \cap B) \cup (A \cap C)$ and $A \cup (B \cap C) = (A \cup B) \cap (A \cup C)$.

Complement of a Set

The **complement** of a set is a set containing all the elements that are *not* in the original set. To determine this, we must also define the **universe of discourse**—the set of all possible elements we're considering, abbreviated U. For mathematical applications, the universe of discourse is commonly the set of all integers (abbreviated $\mathbb{Z}$), or the set of all real numbers (abbreviated $\mathbb{R}$). If U is the set of all integers, for example, then the complement of the set $A = \{1,2,3\}$ would include elements such as -3, 0, or 6, but it would not include elements such as $\sqrt{7}$ or $\frac{1}{4}$, because these are not in the universe of discourse.

The complement of a set is often written either by drawing a line over the name of the original set, or by adding an apostrophe or a superscripted C. The complement of set A, for instance, could be written as $\bar{A}$, as A', or as A^C.

For example, given set $A = \{2,4,6,8\}$ with a universe of discourse of $U = \{1,2,3,4,5,6,7,8,9,10\}$, the complement of set A would be $\{1,3,5,7,9,10\}$—all the elements of U that are not in A.

Difference of Two Sets

The **difference of two sets** is a set containing all the elements that are in the first set but not in the second. The difference of sets A and B is also referred to as the **relative complement** of set A with respect to set B, and is written $A \setminus B$ or $A - B$. The difference is always a subset of the first set: $A \setminus B \subseteq A$. However, it is *not* necessarily the case that $A \setminus B \subseteq B$. In fact, because any element of $A \setminus B$ is by definition not an element of B, the only time that $A \setminus B$ can be a subset of B is if $A \setminus B$ has no elements (i.e., if $A \setminus B = \emptyset$, which is true if and only if, $A \subseteq B$).

Unlike the union and intersection, the operation of the difference between sets is neither commutative nor associative. In general, $A \setminus B \neq B \setminus A$, and $A \setminus (B \setminus C) \neq (A \setminus B) \setminus C$.

For example, consider the sets $A = \{1, 2, 3\}$, $B = \{2, 4\}$, and $C = \{1, 2\}$. Then $A \setminus B = \{1, 3\}$ since 1 and 3 are in set A but not in set B. Similarly, $B \setminus A = \{4\}$, $B \setminus C = \{4\}$, $C \setminus B = \{1\}$, and $A \setminus C = \{3\}$. However, $C \setminus A = \emptyset$, meaning set C is a subset of set A, so there are no elements that appear in C but not in A, which means the difference between C and A is the empty set.

Symbols for Sets Commonly Used in Mathematics

Certain sets are used frequently enough in mathematics to have their own symbols. The standard symbols for these sets resemble upper-case letters of the Latin alphabet, but in a typeface with double lines. Among the most commonly used **sets** are:

- $\mathbb{R}$ – the set of all real numbers
- $\mathbb{Z}$ – the set of all integers
- $\mathbb{N}$ – the set of all natural numbers
- $\mathbb{Q}$ – the set of all rational numbers (numbers that can be written as the ratio of two integers, $\frac{p}{q}$, where $q \neq 0$)
- $\mathbb{C}$ – the set of all complex numbers (numbers of the form $a + bi$, where a and b are real numbers and $i = \sqrt{-1}$)

A superscripted plus or minus sign is used to restrict the set to positive or negative numbers. for instance, $\mathbb{R}^+$ would be the set of all positive real numbers, and $\mathbb{Z}^-$ would be the set of all negative integers.

Some of these sets are, of course, subsets of others. Specifically, $\mathbb{N} \subset \mathbb{Z} \subset \mathbb{Q} \subset \mathbb{R} \subset \mathbb{C}$.

Representing Sets with Recursive and Explicit Formulas

Sets of numbers can have a consistent relationship between the elements of the set. Some of these relationships can be represented with simple recursive or explicit formulas. For example, consider the set of all positive, even numbers (a) and the set of all positive, odd numbers (b):

Positive, Even Numbers:

Recursive: $a_n = a_{n-1} + 2, n \geq 2, a_1 = 0$
Explicit: $a_n = 2n, n \geq 0$

Positive, Odd Numbers:

Recursive: $b_n = b_{n-1} + 2, n \geq 2, b_1 = 1$
Explicit: $b_n = 2n + 1, n \geq 0$

Each set of numbers represents a linear function, with a constant rate of change of 2. The positive, even numbers represent a linear function that is proportional, whereas the positive, odd numbers represent a linear function that is not proportional. The set of even, positive numbers is represented by a function with a y-intercept of 0. The set of odd, positive numbers is represented by a function with a y-intercept of 1.

Set Operations with Venn Diagrams

A **Venn diagram** is a useful visual tool for representing two or three sets and their common elements. Each set is drawn as a **circle**, with the different circles overlapping. Elements are placed in the circle corresponding to the appropriate set or sets—or placed outside all the circles if they belong to the universe of discourse but not to any of the sets.

For example, suppose our universe of discourse is the integers from 1 to 9, and we have the three sets $A = \{1, 2, 3, 4, 5, 6\}$, $B = \{4, 5, 6, 7\}$, and $C = \{3, 6, 9\}$. This could be illustrated with the following Venn diagram:

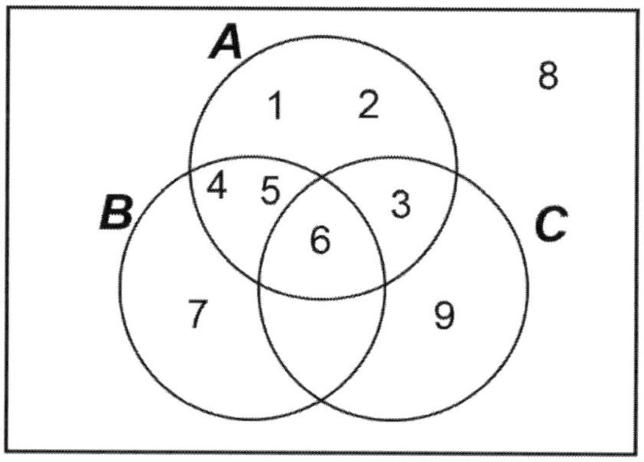

Note, for example, that 6 appears in the center of the diagram where all three circles overlap, because it is an element of all three sets. On the other hand, 8 is placed outside the three circles because it is not an element of any of the sets. Sometimes, instead of writing the elements themselves in the diagram, the total *number* of elements in each part of the Venn diagram is noted. This is especially useful for solving problems involving these numbers of elements.

Using Venn Diagrams to Solve Problems

Venn diagrams are useful for solving problems involving the numbers of elements in sets and in their intersections. By putting those numbers into a Venn diagram, it's simple to see how many must be in the "leftover" parts.

For example, suppose we're told that 200 voters were polled about two propositions, Proposition 1 and Proposition 2. Further, 120 support Proposition 1, 85 support Proposition 2, and 50 support both propositions. To find how many of the voters support neither proposition, we can draw a Venn diagram with a circle representing the supporters of each proposition. We know 50 voters support both propositions, so we can write a 50 in the center of the diagram.

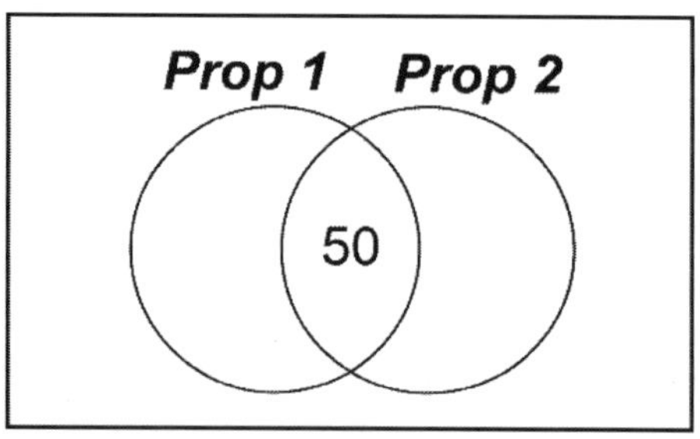

The Proposition 1 circle should contain 120 voters total, so subtracting the 50 voters in the overlap, the other section of the circle must contain $120 - 50 = 70$. Similarly, the nonoverlapping part of the Proposition 2 circle should contain $85 - 50 = 35$.

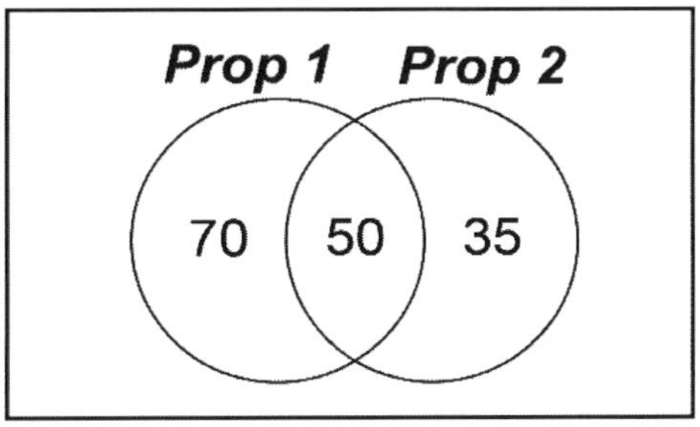

Adding all three sections, the total number of voters supporting either proposition is $70 + 50 + 35 = 155$, so there must be $200 - 155 = 45$ voters who support neither.

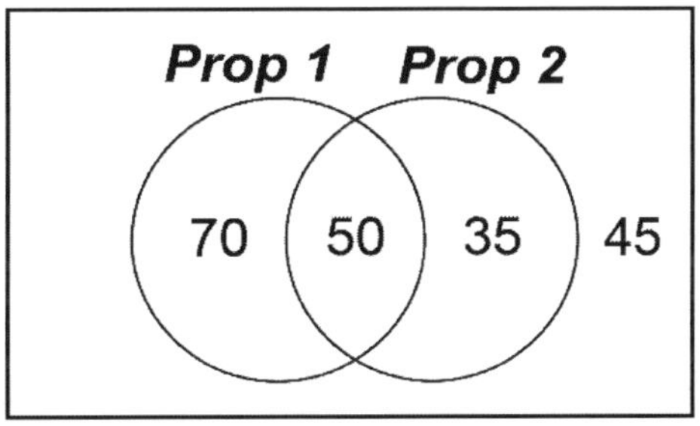

Properties of Infinite Sets

An **infinite set** has an infinite number of elements. A more technical definition is that a set is **infinite** if its elements can be put in one-to-one correspondence with the elements of one of its proper subsets. For instance, consider the set of all positive integers, $\mathbb{Z}^+$. If we remove the number 1, we can still match up every positive integer to an element of the remaining subset (by matching the number n to the number $n + 1$). $\mathbb{Z}^+$ is therefore an infinite set.

The union of an infinite set and any other set is always infinite. The intersection of two infinite sets may or may not be infinite. For instance, consider the set P of prime numbers, the set O of positive odd integers, and the set E of positive even integers—all infinite sets. $P \cap O$ is another infinite set, because there are infinitely many odd prime numbers. $P \cap E$ is finite, because there is only one even prime number. $E \cap O$ is the empty set. Likewise, the complement of an infinite set may be infinite, finite, or the empty set (if the set equals the universe of discourse).

Cardinality

Although all infinite sets have infinitely many members, they may still have different sizes. Two sets are defined as having the same size—or more technically the same **cardinality**—if each element of one set can be matched up to a unique element of the other, with none left over. For example, the set of all integers, $\mathbb{Z}$, and the set of all *even* integers have the same cardinality, even though the latter is a proper subset of the former: every number n in $\mathbb{Z}$ can be matched to a unique number $2n$ in the set of all *even* integers. Although it's more difficult to prove, the set of all rational numbers, $\mathbb{Q}$, also has the same cardinality as $\mathbb{Z}$. However, the set of all real numbers, $\mathbb{R}$, does *not* have the same cardinality—it is impossible to match each integer to a unique real number without any real numbers left over. The most famous proof of this fact was developed by Georg Cantor, and is called the *diagonal argument*.

Sets with the same cardinality as $\mathbb{Z}$ are said to be "countably infinite," or simply **countable**. Sets with a larger cardinality are said to be "uncountably infinite," or **uncountable**.

Practice

P1. Given the sets $X = \{1, 2, 3, 4, 5\}$, $Y = \{2, 4, 6, 8\}$, and $Z = \{1, 3, 7, 13, 21\}$ find the following:

(a) $X \cup Y$

(b) $X \cap Y$

(c) $X \cup (Y \cap Z)$

(d) $(X \cup Y) \cap Z$

Practice Solutions

P1. (a) The union operation includes all elements of the sets being operated on. Thus:

$$X \cup Y = \{1, 2, 3, 4, 5, 6, 8\}$$

(b) The intersection operation includes only elements in both sets being operated on. Thus:

$$X \cap Y = \{2, 4\}$$

(c) First, find the intersection of Y and Z:

$$Y \cap Z = \{\emptyset\}$$

Then, since the intersection of Y and Z is the null set, the union with X is just the elements of X:

$$X \cup (Y \cap Z) = \{1, 2, 3, 4, 5\}$$

(d) First, find the union of X and Y:

$$X \cup Y = \{1, 2, 3, 4, 5, 6, 8\}$$

Then, the intersection of $X \cup Y$ with Z is:

$$(X \cup Y) \cap Z = \{1, 3\}$$

Permutations

For any given set of data, the individual elements in the set may be arranged in different groups containing different numbers of elements arranged in different orders. For example, given the set of integers from one to three, inclusive, the elements of the set are 1, 2, and 3: written as $\{1, 2, 3\}$. They may be arranged as follows: 1, 2, 3, 12, 21, 13, 31, 23, 32, 123, 132, 213, 231, 312, and 321. These ordered sequences of elements from the given set of data are called **permutations**. It is important to note that in permutations, the order of the elements in the sequence is important. The sequence 123 is not the same as the sequence 213. Also, no element in the given set may be used more times as an element in a permutation than it appears as an element in the original set. For example, 223 is not a permutation in the above example because the number 2 only appears one time in the given set.

To find the number of permutations of r items from a set of n items, use the formula ${}_nP_r = \frac{n!}{(n-r)!}$. When using this formula, each element of r must be unique. Also, this assumes that different arrangements of the same set of elements yields different outcomes. For example, 123 is not the same as 321; order is important.

A special case arises while finding the number of possible permutations of n items from a set of n items. Because $n = r$, the equation for the number of permutations becomes simply $P = n!$ The same result is true for $r = n - 1$. Both of these cases are a result of the fact that 0! and 1! are both equal to 1.

If a set contains one or more groups of **indistinguishable or interchangeable elements** (e.g., the set $\{1, 2, 3, 3\}$, which has a group of two indistinguishable 3's), there is a different formula for finding distinct permutations of all n elements. Use the formula $P = \frac{n!}{m_1!m_2!...m_k!}$, where P is the number of permutations, n is the total number of elements in the set, and m_1 through m_k are the number of identical elements in each group (e.g., for the set $\{1, 1, 2, 2, 2, 3, 3\}$, $m_1 = 2$, $m_2 = 3$, and $m_3 = 2$). It is important to note that each repeated number is counted as its own element for the purpose of defining n (e.g., for the set $\{1, 1, 2, 2, 2, 3, 3\}$, $n = 7$, not 3).

To find the number of possible permutations of **any number of elements** in a set of unique elements, you must apply the permutation formulas multiple times. For example, to find the total number of possible permutations of the set $\{1, 2, 3\}$ first apply the permutation formula for situations where $n = r$ as follows: $P = n! = 3! = 6$. This gives the number of permutations of the three elements when all three elements are used. To find the number of permutations when only two of the three elements are used, use the formula ${}_nP_r = \frac{n!}{(n-r)!}$, where n is 3 and r is 2.

$$ {}_nP_r = \frac{n!}{(n-r)!} \Rightarrow {}_3P_2 = \frac{3!}{(3-2)!} = \frac{6}{1} = 6 $$

To find the number of permutations when one element is used, use the formula ${}_nP_r = \frac{n!}{(n-r)!}$, where n is 3 and r is 1.

$$ {}_nP_r = \frac{n!}{(n-r)!} \Rightarrow {}_3P_1 = \frac{3!}{(3-1)!} = \frac{3!}{2!} = \frac{6}{2} = 3 $$

Find the sum of the three formulas: $6 + 6 + 3 = 15$ total possible permutations.

Alternatively, the general formula for total possible permutations can be written as follows:

$$ P_T = \sum_{i=1}^{n} \frac{n!}{(i-1)!} $$

COMBINATIONS

Combinations are essentially defined as permutations where the order in which the elements appear does not matter. Going back to the earlier example of the set $\{1, 2, 3\}$, the possible combinations that can be made from that set are 1, 2, 3, 12, 13, 23, and 123.

In a set containing n elements, the number of combinations of r items from the set can be found using the formula ${}_nC_r = \frac{n!}{r!(n-r)!}$. Notice the similarity to the formula for permutations. In effect, you are dividing the number of permutations by $r!$ to get the number of combinations, and the formula may be written ${}_nC_r = \frac{{}_nP_r}{r!}$. When finding the number of combinations, it is important to remember that the elements in the set must be unique (i.e., there must not be any duplicate items), and that no item may be used more than once in any given sequence.

Review Video: Probability: Permutation and Combination
Visit mometrix.com/academy and enter code: 907664

Practice

P1. Ichiro has 4 shirts, 1 jacket, and 5 different pairs of pants that he packed for his work trip. If wearing a jacket is optional, how many outfit combinations can he make?

P2. Determine the number of permutations and combinations of the following:

(a) Choose 3 from the set: $\{4, 5, 6, 7\}$

(b) Choose 2 from the set: $\{a, b, c, d, e\}$

(c) Choose 4 from the set: $\{a, h, m, t\}$

Practice Solutions

P1. To start with, each shirt can be matched with each pair of pants, so that would be $4 \times 5 = 20$ combinations. Since the jacket is optional each of the 20 can be either with or without the jacket (i.e., $20 \times 2 = 40$). There are 40 distinct combinations he could wear.

P2. (a) ${}_n\text{P}_r = \frac{n!}{(n-r)!} = \frac{4!}{(4-3)!} = \frac{4\times3\times2\times1}{1} = 24$; ${}_n\text{C}_r = \frac{n!}{(n-r)!r!} = \frac{4!}{(4-3)!3!} = \frac{4\times3\times2\times1}{3\times2\times1} = 4$

(b) ${}_n\text{P}_r = \frac{n!}{(n-r)!} = \frac{5!}{(5-2)!} = \frac{5\times4\times3\times2\times1}{3\times2\times1} = 20$; ${}_n\text{C}_r = \frac{n!}{(n-r)!r!} = \frac{5!}{(5-2)!2!} = \frac{5\times4\times3\times2\times1}{(3\times2\times1)\times(2\times1)} = 10$

(c) ${}_n\text{P}_r = \frac{n!}{(n-r)!} = \frac{4!}{(4-4)!} = \frac{4\times3\times2\times1}{1} = 24$; ${}_n\text{C}_r = \frac{n!}{(n-r)!r!} = \frac{4!}{(4-4)!4!} = \frac{4\times3\times2\times1}{1\times(4\times3\times2\times1)} = 1$

Premise and Argument

A **premise** is a statement that precedes a conclusion in an **argument**. It is the proposition, or assumption, of an argument. An argument will have two or more premises.

Example:

If it is hot, then I will go swimming. (Premise)
It is hot. (Premise)
Therefore, I will go swimming. (Conclusion)

Simple and Compound Statements

A **statement** in propositional logic is any sentence or expression that has a truth value—that is, that may in principle be considered true or false. "Hello," for example, is not a statement; there's no sense in which it could be considered true or false. On the other hand, "$2 = 3$" is a statement, albeit a clearly false one. A **compound statement** is a statement that contains one or more other statements, combined or modified in some way. A **simple statement**, or a **proposition**, is a statement that cannot be broken down further into smaller statements.

For example, consider the statement, "If it rains tomorrow, then the streets will be flooded and traffic will be slow." This is a compound statement, because two smaller statements are embedded within it: "it rains tomorrow" and "the streets will be flooded and traffic will be slow." the former cannot be broken down further, and is therefore a simple statement, but the latter is another compound statement, because it includes two simple statements: "the streets will be flooded" and "traffic will be slow."

Common operations used to combine and modify simple statements into compound statements include conjunction, disjunction, negation, and implication.

Conjunction

Conjunction is an operation that combines two or more statements into a compound statement that is true if and only if all of the component statements are true. When the statements are written out, conjunction is marked by the word "and." For example, the statement "Roses are red and violets are blue" is a compound statement that is a conjunction of the two simple statements "roses are red" and "violets are blue."

Conjunction is represented by the operator $\wedge$. In the previous example, if proposition P is "roses are red" and proposition Q is "violets are blue," then the compound statement "roses are red and violets are blue" would be written as "$P \wedge Q$."

Disjunction

Disjunction is an operation that combines two or more statements into a compound statement that is true if and only if at least one of the component statements is true. When the statements are written out, disjunction is marked by the word "or." For example, the statement "I'll clean the closet today, or you'll clean it tomorrow" is a compound statement that is a disjunction of the simple statements "I'll clean the closet today" and "you'll clean the closet tomorrow."

Disjunction is represented by the operator $\vee$. In the previous example, if proposition P is "I'll clean the closet today" and proposition Q is "you'll clean the closet tomorrow," then the compound statement "I'll clean the closet today, or you'll clean it tomorrow" would be written as "$P \vee Q$."

Note that while in everyday language "or" implies exclusivity, as one or the other option but not both, in formal logic disjunction includes the possibility of both propositions being true. If I clean the closet today *and* you clean it tomorrow, then the sample statement "I'll clean the closet today, or you'll clean it tomorrow" is still true.

Conditional and Biconditional Statements

A conditional statement, or **implication**, is a compound statement of the form "if P, then Q." for instance, the statement "if a snake has rattles, then it's venomous" is a conditional statement. It can also be written "P implies Q" ("that a snake has rattles implies that it's venomous") or "P only if Q" ("a snake has rattles only if it's venomous"). The conditional statement is true when both P and Q are true, and even when P is false, regardless of Q. In other words, the conditional statement is false only when P is true and Q is false. The conditional statement is written as "$P \rightarrow Q$." P is called the **premise** of the statement, and Q the **conclusion**.

A **biconditional statement** is a combination of two conditional statements: both "if P, then Q" and "if Q, then P." To state it more concisely, "P if and only if Q." an example is "A number is even if and only if it is divisible by 2." The biconditional statement is true when P and Q are either both true or both false; it is false if P is true and Q is false or vice versa. The biconditional statement is written "$P \leftrightarrow Q$."

Existential and Universal Quantifiers

A **quantifier** is a logical construct used in a compound statement to give information on the number of subjects for which a statement is true. The **existential quantifier** specifies that the statement is true for at least one subject. It is usually introduced as "there exists," such as "there exists a real number that is equal to its own square." The symbol ∃ is used to signify the existential quantifier. For example, the preceding statement could be written as "$\exists x \in \mathbb{R}\; x = x^2$." The **universal quantifier** specifies that the statement is true for *every* subject. It is usually said as "all" or "for all", such as "all real numbers are less than their own squares plus one." The symbol ∀ is used to signify the universal quantifier. For example, the preceding statement could be written as

$$\forall x \in \mathbb{R}\; x < x^2 + 1$$

Sometimes it is useful to specify that there exists *exactly* one subject that meets a given criterion. In other words, there exists a *unique* such subject. This can be signified by adding an exclamation mark after the existential quantifier: "$\exists!\, x \in \mathbb{R}\; |x| = 0$" means "there exists a unique real number that has an absolute value of zero."

Truth Tables

A **truth table** shows the truth value of one or more compound statements for each possible combination of truth values of the propositions within it. The truth table contains one column for each **proposition**, and one column for each of the **compound statements** to be analyzed. It has one row for each combination of **truth values** of the propositions. Since each proposition has two possible truth values, the number of possible combinations for N propositions is 2^N, so the truth table will have 2^N rows.

The table below is a simple truth table for some common compound statements involving two propositions.

P	Q	$P \wedge Q$	$P \vee Q$	$\neg P$	$\neg Q$	$P \to Q$	$Q \to P$	$P \leftrightarrow Q$
T	**T**	**T**	**T**	F	F	**T**	**T**	**T**
T	F	F	**T**	F	**T**	F	**T**	F
F	**T**	F	**T**	**T**	F	**T**	F	F
F	F	F	F	**T**	**T**	**T**	**T**	**T**

Truth tables are useful for comparing two compound statements to see if they are equivalent. They are also useful for analyzing whether complicated compound statements are true or false. A table can have a column for each of the increasingly complex compound statements that combine to form the total statement.

Review Video: Truth Tables
Visit mometrix.com/academy and enter code: 293095

Truth Table to Validate the Rule of Detachment

The **Rule of Detachment** states that given the premises, $P \rightarrow Q$ and P, the valid conclusion is Q.

In other words, for every case where $(P \rightarrow Q) \wedge P$ is true, Q will also be true. The truth table below illustrates this fact:

P	Q	$P \rightarrow Q$	$(P \rightarrow Q) \wedge P$
T	**T**	**T**	**T**
T	F	F	F
F	**T**	**T**	F
F	F	**T**	F

Notice the first cell under $(P \rightarrow Q) \wedge P$ is true, while the first cell under Q is also true. Thus, for every case where $(P \rightarrow Q) \wedge P$ was true, Q was also true.

Truth Table to Validate the Chain Rule

The **Chain Rule** states that given the premises, $P \rightarrow Q$ and $Q \rightarrow R$, the valid conclusion is $P \rightarrow R$.

In other words, for every case where $(P \rightarrow Q) \wedge (Q \rightarrow R)$ is true, $P \rightarrow R$ will also be true. The truth table below illustrates this fact:

P	Q	R	$P \rightarrow Q$	$Q \rightarrow R$	$(P \rightarrow Q) \wedge (Q \rightarrow R)$	$P \rightarrow R$
T	**T**	**T**	**T**	**T**	**T**	**T**
T	**T**	F	**T**	F	F	F
T	F	**T**	F	**T**	F	**T**
T	F	F	F	**T**	F	F
F	**T**	**T**	**T**	**T**	**T**	**T**
F	**T**	F	**T**	F	F	**T**
F	F	**T**	**T**	**T**	**T**	**T**
F	F	F	**T**	**T**	**T**	**T**

Notice that for every case where $(P \rightarrow Q) \wedge (Q \rightarrow R)$ was true, $P \rightarrow R$ was also true.

For example, consider the premises below:

If I hike a mountain, I will not eat a sandwich.
If I do not eat a sandwich, I will drink some water.
I will not drink some water.

Write a valid conclusive statement. Explain how you arrived at your answer. Be specific in your explanation.

Valid conclusive statement: I will not hike a mountain.

Application of the chain rule and rule of contraposition give the valid conclusion of $\neg P$. According to the chain rule, given $P \rightarrow \neg Q$ and $\neg Q \rightarrow R$, then $P \rightarrow R$. According to the rule of contraposition, $P \rightarrow R$ and $\neg R$ yields $\neg P$. On a truth table, for every place where $(P \rightarrow R) \wedge \neg R$ is true, $\neg P$ is also true. Thus, this is a valid conclusive statement.

NEGATION

In propositional logic, **negation** refers to the inversion of the truth value of a statement. The negation of a statement is true if the original statement is false, and false if the original statement is true. Negation can be signified by the word "not." For instance, the negation of the statement "Bob's cat is black" is "Bob's cat is not black." the symbol for negation is $\neg$. So, if the proposition P is "Bob's cat is black," then $\neg P$ would be "Bob's cat is not black." Two negations cancel each other out: $\neg\neg P = P$, or "not not P equals P."

It's important to be careful when combining negation with **quantifiers**. The negation of "there exists a cow that has a blue horn" is not "there exists a cow that does not have a blue horn." Rather, the negation is "there does not exist a cow that has a blue horn." The statements $\neg\exists x\ P(x)$ and $\exists x\ \neg P(x)$ are not equivalent. The same is true for the universal quantifier: $\neg\forall x\ P(x)$ and $\forall x\ \neg P(x)$ do not mean the same thing. There is, however, a connection between the negated quantifiers: $\neg\exists x\ P(x)$ is equivalent to $\forall x\ \neg P(x)$, and $\exists x\ \neg P(x)$ is equivalent to $\neg\forall x\ P(x)$.

Review Video: Negation
Visit mometrix.com/academy and enter code: 429150

DE MORGAN'S LAWS

De Morgan's Laws are a set of useful relations connecting negation, conjunction, and disjunction. They can be stated briefly as "the negation of a conjunction is the disjunction of the negations" and "the negation of a disjunction is the conjunction of the negations." This can be written as:

$$\neg(P \land Q) \leftrightarrow (\neg P) \lor (\neg Q) \text{ and } \neg(P \lor Q) \leftrightarrow (\neg P) \land (\neg Q)$$

For instance, if proposition P is "$x > 3$" and proposition Q is "$y > 3$", then De Morgan's Laws state that "it is not true that both x and y are greater than 3" is equivalent to "either x is not greater than 3, or y is not greater than 3."

The validity of De Morgan's Laws can be shown with truth tables. Note that the columns highlighted in the same color match:

P	Q	$\neg P$	$\neg Q$	$(\neg P) \land (\neg Q)$	$(\neg P) \lor (\neg Q)$	$P \land Q$	$P \lor Q$	$\neg(P \land Q)$	$\neg(P \lor Q)$
T	**T**	F	F	F	F	**T**	**T**	F	F
T	F	F	**T**	F	**T**	F	**T**	**T**	F
F	**T**	**T**	F	F	**T**	F	**T**	**T**	F
F	F	**T**	**T**	**T**	**T**	F	F	**T**	**T**

CONVERSE, INVERSE, AND CONTRAPOSITIVE OF A CONDITIONAL STATEMENT

The **converse** of a **conditional statement** is a conditional statement with the premise and conclusion interchanged. The converse of $P \rightarrow Q$ is $Q \rightarrow P$. The **inverse** has the premise and conclusion both negated. The inverse of $P \rightarrow Q$ is $\neg P \rightarrow \neg Q$. The **contrapositive** has the premise and conclusion both negated *and* interchanged. The contrapositive of $P \rightarrow Q$ is $\neg Q \rightarrow \neg P$.

For example, given the conditional statement, "If there is a key in the lock, then someone is home," the converse is "if someone is home, then there is a key in the lock," the inverse is "if there is not a key in the lock, then no one is home," and the contrapositive is "if no one is home, then there is not a key in the lock."

Note that the converse and inverse of a statement are *not* logically equivalent to the original statement. For instance, the statement "if $x = 4$, then $x > 2$" is true, but its converse "if $x > 2$, then $x = 4$" is not, because there are many numbers greater than 2, not just 4. A statement *is*, however, logically equivalent to its contrapositive. The converse and inverse, while not equivalent to the original statement, are equivalent to each other. The following truth table summarizes the relationships:

P	Q	$\neg P$	$\neg Q$	$P \rightarrow Q$ (statement)	$Q \rightarrow P$ (converse)	$\neg P \rightarrow \neg Q$ (inverse)	$\neg Q \rightarrow \neg P$ (contrapositive)
T	**T**	F	F	**T**	**T**	**T**	**T**
T	F	F	**T**	F	**T**	**T**	F
F	**T**	**T**	F	**T**	F	F	**T**
F	F	**T**	**T**	**T**	**T**	**T**	**T**

Review Video: Converse, Inverse, and Contrapositive
Visit mometrix.com/academy and enter code: 822844

Inductive Reasoning

Inductive reasoning is a method used to make a conjecture, based on patterns and observations. The conclusion of an inductive argument may be true or false.

Mathematical Example:

A cube has 6 faces, 8 vertices, and 12 edges. A square pyramid has 5 faces, 5 vertices, and 8 edges. A triangular prism has 5 faces, 6 vertices, and 9 edges. Thus, the sum of the numbers of faces and vertices, minus the number of edges, will always equal 2, for any solid.

Non-Mathematical Example:

Almost all summer days in Tucson are hot. It is a summer day in Tucson. Therefore, it will probably be hot.

Deductive Reasoning

Deductive reasoning is a method that proves a hypothesis or set of premises. The conclusion of a valid deductive argument will be true, given that the premises are true. Deductive reasoning utilizes logic to determine a conclusion. For instance, consider the following application of the chain rule:

If a ding is a dong, then a ping is a pong.	$p \rightarrow q$
If a ping is a pong, then a ring is a ting.	$q \rightarrow r$
A ding is a dong.	p
Therefore, a ring is a ting.	$\therefore r$

Formal Reasoning

Formal reasoning, in mathematics, involves justification using formal steps and processes to arrive at a conclusion. Formal reasoning is utilized when writing proofs and using logic. For example, when applying logic, validity of a conclusion is determined by truth tables. A set of premises will yield a given conclusion. This type of thinking is formal reasoning. Writing a geometric proof also employs formal reasoning. Example:

If a quadrilateral has four congruent sides, it is a rhombus.
If a shape is a rhombus, then the diagonals are perpendicular.
A quadrilateral has four congruent sides.

Therefore, the diagonals are perpendicular.

Informal Reasoning

Informal reasoning, in mathematics, uses patterns and observations to make conjectures. The conjecture may be true or false. Several, or even many, examples may show a certain pattern, shedding light on a possible conclusion. However, informal reasoning does not provide a justifiable conclusion. A conjecture may certainly be deemed as likely or probable. However, informal reasoning will not reveal a certain conclusion. Consider the following example:

Mathematical Idea – Given a sequence that starts with 1 and each term decreases by a factor of $\frac{1}{2}$, the limit of the sum of the sequence will be 2.

Informal Reasoning – The sum of 1 and $\frac{1}{2}$ is $1\frac{1}{2}$. The sum of 1, $\frac{1}{2}$, and $\frac{1}{4}$ is $1\frac{3}{4}$. The sum of 1, $\frac{1}{2}$, $\frac{1}{4}$, and $\frac{1}{8}$ is $1\frac{7}{8}$. Thus, it appears as the sequence approaches infinity, the sum of the sequence approaches 2.

Proofs

A **proof** serves to show the deductive or inductive process that relates the steps leading from a hypothesis to a conclusion. A proof may be direct ($p \rightarrow q$), meaning that a conclusion is shown to be true, given a hypothesis. There are also proofs by contradiction ($p \wedge {\sim}q$), whereby the hypothesis is assumed to be true, and the negation of the conclusion is assumed to be true. (In other words, the statement is assumed to be false.) Proofs by contraposition (${\sim}q \rightarrow {\sim}p$) show that the negation of the conclusion leads to the negation of the hypothesis. (In other words, the negation of the conclusion is assumed to be true, and it must be shown that the negation of the hypothesis is also true.) A mathematical induction proof seeks to show that $P(1)$ is true and that $P(k+1)$ is true, given that $P(k)$ is true. Direct proofs, proofs by contradiction, and proofs by contraposition use deductive methods, while a mathematical induction proof uses an inductive method.

Direct proofs are those that assume a statement to be true. The purpose of such a proof is to show that the conclusion is true, given that the hypothesis is true. A sample of a direct proof is shown below:

Prove "If m divides a and m divides b, then m divides $a + b$."

Proof:

- Assume m divides a and m divides b.
- Thus, a equals the product of m and some integer factor, p, by the definition of division, and b equals the product of m and some integer factor, q, by the definition of division. According to substitution, $a + b$ may be rewritten as $(m \times p) + (m \times q)$. Factoring out the m gives $m(p + q)$. Since m divides $p + q$, and $p + q$ is an integer, according to the closure property, we have shown that m divides $a + b$, by the definition of division.

Indirect proofs (or proofs by contradiction) are those that assume a statement to be false. The purpose of such a proof is to show that a hypothesis is false, given the negation of the conclusion, indicating that the conclusion must be true. A sample of an indirect proof is shown below:

Prove "If $3x + 7$ is odd, then x is even."

Proof:

- Assume $3x + 7$ is odd and x is odd.
- According to the definition of odd, $x = 2a + 1$, where a is an element of the integers.
- Thus, by substitution, $3x + 7 = 3(2a + 1) + 7$, which simplifies as $6a + 3 + 7$, or $6a + 10$, which may be rewritten as $2(3a + 5)$. Any even integer may be written as the product of 2 and some integer, k. Thus, we have shown the hypothesis to be false, meaning that the conditional statement must be true.

A **proof by contraposition** is one written in the form, $\sim Q \rightarrow \sim P$. In other words, a proof by contraposition seeks to show that the negation of Q will yield the negation of P. A sample of a proof by contraposition is shown below:

Prove "If $5x + 7$ is even, then x is odd."

Proof:

- Assume that if x is even, then $5x + 7$ is odd.
- Assume x is even.
- Thus, by the definition of an even integer, $x = 2a$.

By substitution, $5x + 7$ may be rewritten as $5(2a) + 7$, which simplifies as $10a + 7$. This expression cannot be written as the product of 2 and some factor, k. Thus, $5x + 7$ is odd, by definition of an odd integer. So, when $5x + 7$ is even, x is odd, according to contraposition.

A **proof by contradiction** is one written in the form, $p \wedge \sim q$. In other words, a proof by contradiction seeks to show the negation of q will result in a false hypothesis, indicating that the conclusion of the statement, as written, must be true. In other words, the conditional statement of $p \rightarrow q$ is true.

Mathematical Induction Proof Utilizing Inductive Reasoning

A mathematical induction proof utilizes inductive reasoning in its assumption that if $P(k)$ is true, then $P(k + 1)$ is also true. The induction hypothesis is $P(k)$. This step utilizes inductive reasoning because an observation is used to make the conjecture that $P(k + 1)$ is also true.

Example:

For all natural numbers, n, the sum is equal to $(n + 1)\left(\frac{n}{2}\right)$.
Show that $P(1)$ is true.
$1 = (1 + 1)\left(\frac{1}{2}\right)$.
Assume $P(k)$ is true.
$1 + 2 + 3 + 4 + \cdots + k = (k + 1)\left(\frac{k}{2}\right)$.

This previous step is the inductive hypothesis. This hypothesis may be used to write the conjecture that $P(k+1)$ is also true: $(1+2+3+4+\cdots+k)+(k+1)=[(k+1)+1]\left(\frac{k+1}{2}\right)$

$$(k+1)\left(\frac{k}{2}\right)+(k+1)=[(k+1)+1]\left(\frac{k}{2}+\frac{1}{2}\right)$$
$$(k+1)\left(\frac{k}{2}\right)+(k+1)=\left(\frac{k}{2}(k+1)+\frac{k}{2}\right)+\left(\frac{1}{2}(k+1)+\frac{1}{2}(1)\right)$$
$$(k+1)\left(\frac{k}{2}\right)+(k+1)=\frac{k}{2}(k+1)+\frac{k}{2}+\frac{k+1}{2}+\frac{1}{2}$$
$$(k+1)\left(\frac{k}{2}\right)+(k+1)=\frac{k}{2}(k+1)+\frac{2k+2}{2}$$
$$(k+1)\left(\frac{k}{2}\right)+(k+1)=\frac{k}{2}(k+1)+(k+1)$$

PRACTICE

P1. Given the following statements:

If I get a bonus, then I will go on vacation.
If I go on vacation, then I will visit Egypt.
I got a bonus.

Therefore, I will visit Egypt.

(a) Rewrite the statements in logical notation.

(b) Make a truth table for the scenario.

(c) Determine if the argument is logical.

(d) TRUE or FALSE: It would contradict this argument to visit Egypt and not have received a bonus.

P2. Given the following statements:

I will run a marathon in January if and only if the Cubs win the World Series.
I will not run a marathon in January.

Therefore, the Cubs did not win the World Series.

(a) Rewrite the statements in logical notation.

(b) Make a truth table for the scenario.

(c) Determine if the argument is logical.

(d) TRUE or FALSE: It is logically equivalent to the first premise above to say, "I will not run a marathon in January if and only if the Cubs do not win the World Series.

P3. Use proof by induction to demonstrate: "The sum of n odd natural numbers is equal to n^2."

P4. Use informal reasoning to justify the statement, "If n is a whole number, then $n^2 + n + 1$ is odd." Explain the reasoning steps used.

P5. Use formal reasoning to justify the statement, "If a divides b, a divides c, and a divides d, then a divides the sum of b, c, and d." Show the formal proof.

Practice Solutions

P1. (a) Let us say "getting a bonus" $= B$, "going on vacation" $= V$, and "visiting Egypt" $= E$:

If I get a bonus, then I will go on vacation.	$B \to V$
If I go on vacation, then I will visit Egypt.	$V \to E$
I got a bonus.	B
Therefore, I will visit Egypt.	$\therefore E$

(b) The truth table for the scenario:

B	V	E	$B \to V$	$V \to E$	$(B \to V) \land (V \to E)$	$B \to E$
T	**T**	**T**	**T**	**T**	**T**	**T**
T	**T**	F	**T**	F	F	F
T	F	**T**	F	**T**	F	**T**
T	F	F	F	**T**	F	F
F	**T**	**T**	**T**	**T**	**T**	**T**
F	**T**	F	**T**	F	F	**T**
F	F	**T**	**T**	**T**	**T**	**T**
F	F	F	**T**	**T**	**T**	**T**

(c) This is an instance of the chain rule and is logically sound.

(d) FALSE: It would NOT contradict this argument to visit Egypt and not have received a bonus. Look at the rows of the truth table where $B =$ F and $E =$ T, in these cases both statements hold:

B	V	E	$B \to V$	$V \to E$	$(B \to V) \land (V \to E)$	$B \to E$
F	**T**	**T**	**T**	**T**	**T**	**T**
F	F	**T**	**T**	**T**	**T**	**T**

P2. (a) Let us say "Cubs win" $= C$ and "running a marathon" $= M$:

I will run a marathon in January if and only if the Cubs win the World Series.	$C \leftrightarrow M$
I will not run a marathon in January.	$\neg M$
Therefore, the Cubs did not win the World Series.	$\therefore \neg C$

(b) The truth table for the scenario:

C	M	$\neg C$	$\neg M$	$C \leftrightarrow M$	$C \leftrightarrow (M \land \neg M)$	$\neg M \to \neg C$
T	**T**	F	F	**T**	F	**T**
T	F	F	**T**	F	F	F
F	**T**	**T**	F	F	**T**	**T**
F	F	**T**	**T**	**T**	**T**	**T**

(c) Based on the truth table, it is clear that $C \leftrightarrow (M \land \neg M)$ is logically equivalent to $\neg C$.

(d) TRUE: The following truth table demonstrates the equivalence:

C	M	$\neg C$	$\neg M$	$C \leftrightarrow M$	$\neg M \leftrightarrow \neg C$
T	**T**	F	F	**T**	**T**
T	F	F	**T**	F	F
F	**T**	**T**	F	F	F
F	F	**T**	**T**	**T**	**T**

P3. Show that $P(1)$ is true.

$$1 = 1^2.$$

Assume $P(k)$ is true.

$$1 + 3 + 5 + \cdots + (2k + 1) = k^2.$$

We want to show that $1 + 3 + 5 + \cdots + (2(k + 1) + 1) = (k + 1)^2$.

$$1 + 3 + 5 + \cdots + (2k + 1) + [2k + 1] = k^2 + [2k + 1].$$

We can distribute 2 to each of the k terms:

$$(1 + 2) + (3 + 2) + (5 + 2) + \cdots + (2k + 1 + 2) + [1] = k^2 + [2k + 1].$$

$$3 + 5 + 7 + \cdots + \big((2k + 2) + 1\big) + [1] = k^2 + 2k + 1.$$

Rearrange and simplify:

$$1 + 3 + 5 + 7 + \cdots + (2(k + 1) + 1) = (k + 1)^2.$$

$P(k + 1)$ is true. Thus, according to mathematical induction,

$$1 + 3 + 5 + \cdots + (2n + 1) = n^2.$$

P4. Using the sequence, 0, 1, 2, 3, 4, 5, 6, ... for n, evaluation of the expression, $n^2 + n + 1$, gives $0^2 + 0 + 1$, $1^2 + 1 + 1$, $2^2 + 2 + 1$, $3^2 + 3 + 1$, $4^2 + 4 + 1$, $5^2 + 5 + 1$, and $6^2 + 6 + 1$, or 1, 3, 7, 13, 21, 31, and 43, all of which are odd numbers. Thus, it appears that given any whole number, n, evaluation of the expression $n^2 + n + 1$ will yield an odd number.

P5. Direct Proof:

Assume a divides b, a divides c, and a divides d.

Given the definition of divides, a divides b indicates that there exists some integer, r, such that $b = a \times r$. Also, a divides c indicates that there exists some integer, s, such that $c = a \times s$. Finally, a divides d indicates that there exists some integer, t, such that $d = a \times t$. By substitution, the sum of b, c, and d may be written as $(a \times r) + (a \times s) + (a \times t)$. Factoring out an a gives $a(r + s + t)$. The factor $(r + s + t)$ is an integer, according to the closure property under addition. Thus, a divides the sum of b, c, and d.

Digital Forensics

Digital Forensic Tools and Cyberattacks

When network traffic is monitored on a regular basis, patterns in the data typically emerge. This is usually observable by certain amounts of traffic at certain times of day. Digital forensic tools can be used to analyze the network traffic and paint a clear picture of these patterns. Use of these tools also allows for quick identification of anomalies in the traffic. An anomaly in the traffic pattern can signal multiple things, including a potential cyberattack. Further investigation into the cause would be required. Additional digital forensic tools can be used in the investigation to allow the network owner to obtain more details about the traffic and determine whether a cyberattack is occurring.

Digital Forensics in Law Enforcement

There are many ways that digital forensics is used in law enforcement today. Since digital devices are used in almost every aspect of a person's life, there is a large trail of a person's activity left on these devices. Law enforcement may obtain warrants to recover a suspect's internet search history, computer files, or other data that may act as evidence of a crime. In addition to recovering data, digital forensics can even be used to obtain a history of the suspect's location. If the person has a cell phone, history from cell towers can be obtained to determine the exact location of the person at a specific day and time. This type of evidence is not always used to obtain a conviction. It can also be used to exonerate a suspect.

Data Recovery Businesses

A **data recovery business** uses digital forensic tools on a daily basis. These tools may be used by the business for various reasons. In some cases, it could be very simple. Perhaps a person deleted some files from a computer unintentionally. A data recovery expert may then use a very simple forensic tool to recover the files that were deleted. In other cases, things could get more complicated. Digital forensic experts may work with private investigators to uncover information as part of an investigation. It is also common for a data recovery expert to work closely with law enforcement to use digital forensics to recover evidence as part of a criminal investigation. It is always important for the data recovery business to keep in mind whether or not they have a legal right to obtain the information being requested.

Common Forensic Tools

There are numerous tools that exist today that allow someone to analyze network traffic. Some of these tools are built into most operating systems, others are available for free download, and some are only available through purchase at a premium price. Some built-in command line tools include ipconfig and ping. Ipconfig allows a user to view network information related to the local machine, while ping allows a user to send packets to another machine for testing connectivity. NetDetector and NetIntercept are two very powerful tools that can be used for network analysis. NetDetector analyzes network traffic and observes patterns that may indicate improper network usage. NetIntercept actually captures packets of information as they traverse the network and allows the user to capture files and information passed over the network.

Identifying Malicious Attacks

There are many tools available today that can analyze network traffic data on many levels. Some tools even go all the way down to the packet level, providing specific information and statistics about individual packets being passed over the network. By constantly monitoring this data, network professionals are able to get a good baseline of what normal traffic looks like across their networks. In the event of a malicious attack, the traffic across the network may suddenly spike. This spike would trigger the network team to begin a deeper dive into the data and determine the cause of the spike. The constant monitoring and analysis of the traffic data can assist in identifying an attack more quickly. This allows the network team to respond rapidly, reducing the effects of the attack.

Robotics

Concept of Robotics

Robotics is a rapidly growing field, and there are many uses for robots in the market today. Some robots are trained to perform one very specific task, and they have no real cognitive or decision-making abilities. Others, however, use machine learning or artificial intelligence to make decisions in their work. Robots can actually be physical machines made from hardware, or they can also be implemented completely in software. Hardware robots can be found in manufacturing facilities, warehouses, or even behind the desk at a hotel. Software robots are generally found in office environments where they perform repetitive work on computers. Creating either type of robot requires a strong knowledge of computer science concepts, as the robot must be programmed to perform its work.

System Integration in Robotics

System integration is extremely important in the field of robotics. In many instances, each part of the robot may be considered a separate system. For example, the arms, legs, hands, and head may all be different systems of the robot. In order to function correctly, all of these systems must interact with each other seamlessly. In addition to the robot's internal systems, a robot typically interacts with many external systems. It may gather information from one system and perform work on another system. The ability to interact with many different external systems is critical to its functionality. System integration plays a key role in making sure that the robot is able to monitor its surroundings and respond appropriately.

Prototyping

Robots can be very expensive and time consuming to develop. For this reason, it is generally a good idea to create a **prototype** for testing purposes. This allows the creator to test the design and other features more quickly and at a much lower cost. If there are errors with the prototype, they can be corrected before the final build is completed. A prototype does not necessarily have to include every single detail of the final design. However, it is a great way to test general design concepts and some system integrations. By using prototypes, it is also possible to test multiple designs to determine which one is the best solution for the final product.

Refinement of a Design

Once a prototype has been designed and thoroughly tested, it is then time to move to the final version. It is generally a good idea to conduct multiple tests using prototypes before moving to the final version. Testing multiple times ensures that the best design is selected, and it also minimizes the chance that unexpected issues arise. Any refinements needed as a result of the prototype testing should be implemented at this point. Final details should also be worked out at this time. Since prototype testing generally does not test every single detail of the design, this is when those additional details should be integrated into the design.

Programming and Controlling Robots

Robots must be trained to perform their work. Most of the time, this training consists of a developer writing computer code that the robot will execute. Sometimes, the robot may have a direct interface for this development to occur. This is often the case in a manufacturing environment. A controls engineer can use a terminal to directly access the robot and change its behavior very quickly. In other cases, the robot may have its own onboard memory where instructions are loaded and stored. In these cases, a developer would need to use a computer for the development of the instructions and then transfer the instructions to the robot's internal memory. This can take more time depending on what type of instructions are needed for the robot to understand.

Example Simple Robotics Algorithm

Let's first assume a few things about the robot. Let's assume that the robot has two independent rear wheels used for motion, infrared sensors for identifying special tape, and ultrasonic sensors to prevent it from hitting a wall. We will also assume that the robot has some way of knowing when it has reached the end of the maze. The algorithm may look something like this. While infrared sensor detects tape, move both wheels forward. If no tape is detected, use infrared sensor to determine whether a right or left turn is needed. Rotate right or left wheel forward to make the necessary turn. If ultrasonic sensor detects a wall too close, then rotate wheels backward. Continue to follow these instructions through the maze until the endpoint is reached. When the endpoint is reached, stop rotation of the wheels. The maze is complete.

Applications of Robotics in the Modern World

One of the largest applications for physical robots today is in the manufacturing industry. Robots can be used to perform work that may be too dangerous or physically taxing for a human. Robots are able to lift large amounts of weight and assemble items that a human could not, or they can perform the same tasks faster and more safely. In some cases, the robot works in tandem with a human, making the job safer for the person. There are other instances where the effect on society is not as well received. Robots are sometimes used in customer service roles, either through automated chat sessions or call systems. People often get frustrated with these systems because many prefer to talk to live people instead of robots. In this case, the use of robots can have a negative effect instead of a positive one.

Perspectives on Use of Robotics in Society

Some people feel that the adoption of more robots into the workforce means there will be fewer jobs available for people. Most will agree that having fewer jobs available has a negative impact on society. People worry that some jobs in the labor market will be completely taken over by robots, and the people who perform these jobs today will be left with no opportunities. While this is a legitimate concern, recent research has shown that the emergence of robots in the workplace will actually lead to additional jobs being created, such as new jobs based around robot development, robot maintenance, and other work with the robots themselves. These new skillsets are in high demand, and some educational facilities are attempting to train workers in these new fields.

Game and Mobile Application Development

Differences between Mobile App and Traditional Desktop Development

One big difference between mobile app development and traditional app development is in the requirements. Typically, the requirements of a traditional desktop app are derived from the users of the application. With a mobile app, it is sometimes not as easy to gather requirements from the users. In some cases, the developers may not even know who all of the users will be. Intense research is often needed to determine what features should be included in the mobile app. Another difference is that in mobile app development, a prototype is generally made available to some users for testing purposes and for gathering feedback. In traditional application development, the developers typically design to the specifications and then allow for testing. Feedback is rarely taken into account as long as the specifications are met.

Video Game Design

Career possibilities in **video game design** have increased in recent years with the popularity of video games and new gaming systems. Even smartphones are used for video games today, so the market for video games is constantly increasing. A video game designer is responsible for all aspects of creating the game. The designer creates rules for the game, gameplay details, and even the characters. In some cases, the designer may act as an artist as well by sketching characters or certain items in the game. For larger games, more than one designer may be involved. It is possible to break the overall game down into subsystems, with a different designer working on each subsystem. The designer may or may not actually write code to implement the game. In today's more complex game systems, a separate code developer is usually involved to translate the designer's plans into code.

Graphics Coordinate System and Viewpoints

The graphics coordinate system is very similar to an x,y,z coordinate system in mathematics. In the graphics coordinate system, the coordinates in the x,y plane refer to specific pixels on the screen. A coordinate system such as this is necessary to display images and objects in the game. This applies to both two-dimensional and three-dimensional games. Two of the most popular viewpoints used in 3D games today are first person and third person. A first-person view shows the way that things look from the player character's point of view. For instance, a racecar driver sitting behind the wheel of the racecar sees the track in front of him. A third-person view shows the overall landscape and action of the game from the view of some independent camera. In some cases, such as baseball or football games, there may be multiple camera angles.

Image Rendering

Image rendering is what allows the computer to create three-dimensional images on a flat, two-dimensional display. The computer is able to take a model of the object and convert that into a three-dimensional image. The calculations that are associated with this conversion can get extremely complicated. For this reason, image rendering requires a lot of processing power, particularly in games that require image rendering in real time. Some games must render these images at a rate of 60-144 frames per second. That means that a new image must be created at least once every $1/60^{th}$ of a second. Add in the fact that the rendering must account for light, shadows, and other atmospheric variations, and it is easy to tell why so much processing power is needed for today's graphics-intensive video games.

Video Game User Experience

There are many factors in a video game that affect the experience of the person playing the game. One of the biggest, yet often overlooked factors is the availability of proper instructions. If no instructions are provided, or if the game is simply too complicated to learn, then the user's experience will be negatively impacted. Other considerations are length of the game, difficulty of the game, and how many players are allowed to play at once. Another big factor is the responsiveness of the game. If the game lags, doesn't respond well to controls, or takes too long to render images, then players will likely lose interest.

Advantages of Multiplayer Online Gaming

Having the ability to play a game online with other players from around the world creates a user experience that generally cannot be matched with a local instance of the game. Players feel like they become part of an online community. They become exposed to different strategies for playing the game, and they can learn lots of tips and tricks from other users. Most of the time, forums and discussion boards pop up on the Internet where players can discuss different aspects of the game. Tournaments are even created for some games, allowing players to compete against each other to determine who is the best player. All of these things lead to a positive increase in the user experience, and they also allow for additional revenue streams to the game developer.

Connections with Board Games

Some video games are digital replicas of specific board games, while others closely model some board games. Playing board games can assist with the design and development of video games. First, playing board games can assist video game designers in writing thorough instructions. It allows the designers to see how important the instructions are and identify best practices for writing instructions. Another way that playing board games helps video game development is that it assists in accounting for all possible scenarios in the game. If an unexpected situation occurs in a video game, it is possible that the game could crash. This would be unacceptable to a user, so the developer must account for all possible events during play. Finally, it allows the developers to gain insight into strategy development.

Event-Driven Programming

Event-driven programming allows for the tasks in the program to vary based on some input provided to the system. This input could come from the system itself, another system, or even a human user. Event-driven programming uses things called event listeners and event handlers. These names give insight into their functions. An event listener stores information about each event as it happens. The event handler determines what action needs to be taken based on the specifics of each event. Event-driven programming can become very complex, as some systems have a very large number of events that could occur. It is necessary to account for all of these events so that the program knows how to react when any of them occur.

Traditional development assumes that the process being completed flows in a somewhat linear fashion. The sequence of steps typically goes in the same order each time through, with a few rules-based logical decision exceptions. However, consider a video game and how the game must react to any input provided by the user. In modern video games, it is rare that the same thing will happen multiple times in succession. Rather, each time through the game, things may be slightly different. Event-driven programming allows the developer to handle all of these different events appropriately. The game will react differently based on the action that the user takes. The developer must attempt to account for all possible events that may occur and develop the game so that it can handle all of these different events.

Collision Detection

Collision detection is a way for a computer program, or video game in this case, to determine what will happen when two objects collide with each other. This is important because video game players expect that the objects will generally react the same way as they would in the real world during a collision. For instance, imagine a bowling video game. When the ball is rolled down the lane, collisions occur between the ball and the bowling pins. It's also possible that collisions may occur between some falling pins and other pins that are still upright. The game developer must determine how these collisions will be modeled and whether a pin will fall as a result of the collision. These calculations can become very complex and often rely on reflecting the laws of physics for proper simulations.

Chapter Quiz

Ready to see how well you retained what you just read? Scan the QR code to go directly to the chapter quiz interface for this study guide. If you're using a computer, simply visit the online resources page at **mometrix.com/resources719/texescompsci241** and click the Chapter Quizzes link.

TExES Practice Test

Want to take this practice test in an online interactive format?
Check out the online resources page, which includes interactive practice questions and much more: **mometrix.com/resources719/texescompsci241**

1. In the following recursive method, what precondition must be given to include ALL valid input values for `num` without causing infinite recursion?

```
int calculate(int num)
      if(num == 4)
            return 0
      else if(num > 5 and num ≤ 10)
            return 5 + calculate(num - 1)
      else
            return 10 + calculate(num - 1)
      end if
end calculate
```

a. `num ≤ 4`
b. `num ≥ 4`
c. `num < 4`
d. `num > 4`

2. A school wants to use spreadsheet software to display information about the percentage of students who are getting As, Bs, Cs, Ds, or Fs in a computer science class. Which of the following graphs would be the best to represent this data so that you can easily see the percentage of students in relation to the whole?

a. Bar graph
b. Pie chart
c. Line graph
d. Scatter plot

3. Sarah is trying to program a robot to navigate a maze. She has implemented a simple programming interface in which different colors represent the actions the robot can take.

Blue: move one space in the direction the robot is currently facing
Red: rotate clockwise one quarter-turn
Orange: rotate counterclockwise one quarter-turn

If Sarah's robot is currently facing east, which set of commands will allow her robot to be two squares north of her current position, given that there are no obstacles in sight?

a. Red, Blue, Blue
b. Orange, Orange, Blue, Blue
c. Blue, Red, Red, Blue, Orange, Blue, Blue
d. Blue, Orange, Orange, Blue, Red, Blue, Blue

4. A certain small file type has a maximum size of 7 bytes and 3 bits. If the file is currently 3 bytes and 5 bits, how many more bits can be stored as part of the file?

a. 30 bits
b. 38 bits
c. 3 bits
d. 62 bits

5. Which of the following is a necessary precondition for the following code:

```
if(num ≥ 0)
   total ← total / num
end if
```

a. `num > 0`
b. `num ≠ 0`
c. `num < 0`
d. `num ≥ 0`

6. Imagine that a new programming language named ChitChat has been created. In ChitChat programming, the source code can run on any computer, but the computer needs to be running another piece of software that translates the source code so that it can be understood by the particular computer that it is running on. From the information given, it can be determined that ChitChat is an example of ________.

a. a compiled language
b. an interpreted language
c. an object-oriented language
d. an assembly language

7. The use of code in a step-wise procedure to develop applications is called ________.

a. object-oriented programming
b. procedural programming
c. functional programming
d. low-level programming

8. Given the following Java code, what is contained in `String c`?

```
String sport = "gymnastics";
String a = sport.substring(1, 2);
String b = sport.substring(3, 6);
String c = b + a;
```

a. mnasgy
b. nasy
c. mnag
d. nastgym

9. Which of the following is the correct order of abstraction for software from top to bottom?

a. User, application, operating system, hardware
b. User, operating system, application, hardware
c. User, hardware, application, operating system
d. User, application, hardware, operating system

10. What will be printed when the following Java code is run?

```
String words[] = {"chocolate", "cookie", "Claire",
"Charles"};
int count = 0;
for(int i = 0; i < words.length; i++)
{
     if(words[i].startsWith("C"))
     {
          count += i;
     }
}
System.out.println(count);
```

a. 7
b. 2
c. 5
d. 4

11. A student just finished writing some code for a class project but is getting an error message. Look at the code to identify which error message the student is receiving.

```
void printNames()
     String nameArray ← ["Moe", "Larry", "Curly"]
     int size ← 3
     for(int i ← 0; i ≤ size; i ← i + 1)
          print "Hi " + nameArray[i]
     end for
end printNames
```

a. Null pointer exception
b. Index out of bounds
c. Incompatible types
d. Missing return statement

12. David is configuring his network and wants to purchase hardware that will transmit all information that it receives identically to all computers connected to it. He also wants the cheapest solution to this problem. David should use a ________.

a. router
b. switch
c. hub
d. gateway

13. A random number generator in a computer is never truly random because computers are ________.

a. Deterministic
b. Logic-based
c. Conventional
d. Indiscriminate

14. In an inclusion classroom, a student with profound hearing loss is regularly mocked by students when she speaks. How should the classroom teacher and resource teacher work to solve this issue?

a. Punish the behavior immediately in front of the class.
b. Create and put in place a strict no-bullying policy for all students in the classroom.
c. Move the child back to a self-contained environment for her protection.
d. Contact the parents and guardians of all students to explain what is occurring.

15. When having a parent-teacher conference, who should generally open the conference and state its main purpose?

a. The administrator or school counselor should be the one who starts the conference.
b. The parents should begin the conference because they know what their child needs best.
c. The person who asked for the conference should start the meeting and establish its focus.
d. The teacher should begin the conference because it is the teacher's responsibility.

16. Use the Java class below to answer the following question:

```
public class Card
{
        private String suit = "";
        private int value = 0;

        public Card(String suit, int value)
        {
                this.suit = suit;
                this.value = value;
        }

        public String getSuit()
        {
                return suit;
        }
        public int getValue()
        {
                return value;
        }

        public boolean checkWin()
        {
        }
}
```

In a certain card game, players take turns picking up cards. If the card they pick up is a "diamond" for the suit, and the value is evenly divisible by 2, they win. What code should be placed in the `checkWin()` method?

a.

```
if(Card.getSuit().equals("diamond") && Card.getValue() % 2 == 0)
     return true;
     return false;
```

b.

```
if(Card.getSuit().equals("diamond") && Card.getValue() / 2 == 0)
    return true;
    return false;
```

c.

```
if(getSuit().equals("diamond") && getValue() % 2 == 0)
    return true;
    return false;
```

d.

```
if(getSuit().equals("diamond") && getValue() / 2 == 0)
    return true;
    return false;
```

17. Given the following code, which values of `a` and `b` will cause the expression to evaluate to true?

```
if((a && b) && !(a && FALSE))
```

a. a = true; b = true
b. a = false; b = false
c. a = true; b = false
d. a = false; b = true

18. Which of the following would be a good use of randomization in computing?

a. Randomly generating the cost of an item on a website
b. Randomly generating inventory of a certain item
c. Randomly generating a username for a new user
d. Randomly generating items in a user's shopping cart

19. Jane is writing a program to calculate the area of her garden. Her current garden is 12.5 feet by 14.25 feet. She wrote the following method,

```
1    int gardenArea(float length, float width)
2         float area ← area
3         area ← 12.5 * 14.25
4         return area
5    end gardenArea
```

and then printed it with this:

```
print gardenArea(12.5, 14.25)
```

There are a few mistakes in this program. However, if Jane wanted to create a second garden, which line contains the error that prevents the code from being reusable for new values?

a. Line 1
b. Line 2
c. Line 3
d. Line 4

20. What is the value of `x` after the following Java code executes?

```
double x = Math.pow(2, 3) + 3 * 6 - 4 * (12 - 8) / 2;
```

a. 19.0
b. 136.0
c. 124.0
d. 18.0

21. What is the value of `answer` after the following Java code is run?

```
int x = 5;
int y = 7;
int z = 9;
x++;
z--;
y += z;
x += x;
int answer = z - y + x;
```

a. 5
b. 9
c. 12
d. 18

22. Use the following Java method to answer the question:

```
public static int mystery(int a, int b)
{
    if(a % b > b % a)
        return a % b;
    else
        return b % a;
}
```

What will be printed for the following code?

```
System.out.println(mystery(13, 5));
```

a. 1
b. 0
c. 3
d. 5

23. Which of the following is a reason to write original code instead of using a library?

a. Writing original code is more convenient.
b. Writing original code is less time consuming.
c. Original code is more likely to be bug free.
d. Original code is better suited to unique purposes.

24. A high school robotics team sends the signals below to their robot to control it.

0 forward
1 backward
2 pivot left
3 pivot right

They are worried about other teams picking up their signals to determine how to complete the challenges, so they have encrypted their signals. Below is their decryption key.

```
(input - 2) % 4
```

What actions will the robot take if they send the encrypted commands below to their robot?

```
7, 9, 18, 4
```

a. Pivot right, backward, pivot left, forward
b. Backward, pivot right, forward, forward
c. Backward, pivot right, forward, pivot left
d. Pivot right, backward, pivot left, pivot left

25. A teacher is writing code to add up all the grades for a given class and determine the class average. The grades are stored in an array named `grades[]`. Read the following code and determine what code should replace `/* missing code */` so that the code satisfies its given purpose.

```
float average ← 0
float total ← 0
for(int i ← 0; i < grades.length; i ← i + 1)
     /* missing code */
end for
print average
```

a.
```
total ← total + grades[i]
average ← total / grades.length
```

b.
```
total ← grades[i]
average ← total / grades.length
```

c.
```
average ← total / grades.length
```

d.
```
average ← total / (grades.length + 1)
```

26. Which of the following is a characteristic of a high-level language?

a. Has almost direct communication with hardware
b. Provides little to no abstraction
c. Is CPU-specific
d. Helps deal with memory management

27. Which of the following strategies would most effectively work to meet the multiple learning needs of diverse students?

a. Enforcing a rigid schedule
b. Simplifying content for the whole class
c. Implementing a variety of different instructional daily activities
d. Incorporating more learning games to increase enthusiasm

28. Robert is designing an online store. He negotiated a flat-rate deal with a shipping company: $10 to ship an order anywhere in the United States. In many places in his code, he wrote something similar to this:

```
totalCost ← totalCost + 10
```

in order to calculate the shipping cost. If the shipping charge changes in the future to $12, which of the following methods is the most efficient and correct way to make the change?

a. Use the "find and replace" feature to replace all instances of 10 with 12.
b. Replace all the instances with a constant to represent the shipping cost and set it to 12.
c. Replace all the instances with a variable to represent the shipping cost and set it to 12.
d. Manually search for instances where 10 should be 12 and change the value.

29. A major reason why the base number system in computer systems is binary is because modern computers use ________.

a. Vacuum tubes
b. Integrated circuits
c. Central processing units
d. Transistors

30. Which of the following is an example of citizen science?

a. A small team of researchers analyzing the bird population in a town
b. A scientist analyzing DNA samples in her free time
c. Hikers logging into a global app to report bear sightings
d. Social media internally keeping track of user opinions about global warming

31. David wants to compute the average of three numbers. He writes the code below.

```
double total ← 57 + 22.0 + 81 / 3.0
```

This code results in a _________ error.

a. runtime
b. logic
c. round-off
d. syntax

32. What output will be displayed after the following Java code is run?

```
for(int j = 4; j >= 1; j--)
{
      for(int k = j; k >= 1; k--)
      {
            System.out.print(3 * k - 2);
      }
      System.out.println();
}
```

a.

```
10741
   741
   41
   1
```

b.

```
14710
   147
   14
   1
```

c.

```
10741
```

d.

14710

33. James wants to retrieve a list of numbers from a user and then be able to search for a particular number easily using a binary search. What steps must he complete in order to make this work correctly?

a. Ask for a list of numbers, sort the numbers, ask for a target number, do a binary search
b. Ask for a list of numbers, ask for a target number, do a binary search, sort the numbers
c. Sort the numbers, ask for a list of numbers, ask for a target number, do a binary search
d. Ask for a target number, ask for a list of numbers, do a binary search, sort the numbers

34. Given the following method,

```
double calculate(int number)
    double cost ← 8
    cost ← cost * number
    return cost
end calculate
```

What will be printed when the following code is executed?

```
double cost ← 7
print calculate(5)
print cost
```

a. 40
   40
b. 40
   7
c. 7
   7
d. 40
   8

35. Becky just moved to the neighborhood and discovered that her neighbor's 100 Mbps Wi-Fi signal was not protected. She decides to use this signal as her main source of internet while at home, connecting all her devices to it. Which is the following is a valid consequence of her actions?

a. Becky could be arrested for Wi-Fi signal theft.
b. Her neighbor's Wi-Fi speed will decrease.
c. Her neighbor's ISP will send a notice to Becky.
d. Becky will be more exposed to computer viruses.

36. Which of the following acts as an intermediary between client and web server requests?

a. Compiler
b. Web browser
c. Database
d. SSL

37. Consider the `if` statement below.

```
if(cost ≥ 100)
      print "free shipping"
else if(cost ≥ 50)
      print "$5 shipping"
else
      print "$10 shipping"
end if
```

Which of the following is the smallest set of input values that will sufficiently test all cases and boundaries?

a. 101, 100, 75, 50, 25
b. 150, 75, 25
c. 200
d. 101, 102, 51, 52, 40, 41

38. What will the following loop print?

```
String myString = "ball";
for(int i = 0; i < myString.length(); i = i + 2)
{
      System.out.print(myString.substring(i));
}
```

a. allll
b. al
c. bl
d. ballll

39. Which of the following could NOT be protected by a copyright?

a. Computer code
b. An original painting
c. The idea for a better toaster
d. The blueprint of a house

40. Examine the following code:

```
void calculate(int x, int y)
      int answer
      answer ← answer + 1
      answer ← answer + x / y
      print answer
end calculate
```

The code is meant to display one more than the result of `x` divided by `y`. Which of the following errors will occur when this call is made to calculate?

```
calculate(4, 2)
```

a. Roundoff error
b. Logic error
c. Compile-time error
d. Runtime error

41. The data that populates the portion of a digital clock indicating the meridian (a.m. or p.m.) would most efficiently be represented with which of the following datatypes?

a. A string
b. An integer
c. A float
d. A Boolean

42. Which of the following problems would be best solved using a heuristic approach?

a. determining the total number of purchases made on a website on any given day
b. determining the average number of points a player made per game in a basketball season
c. determining the best streets to turn down to get to a destination while driving
d. determining the largest number in an array

43. Which of the following is NOT a truly random event?

a. Flipping a coin
b. Spinning a roulette wheel
c. Shuffling cards and picking one
d. A computer using a random number generator

44. The Fibonacci sequence is a sequence of numbers where each number is the sum of the two previous numbers. Here is an example of the first 10 numbers:

1 1 2 3 5 8 13 21 34 55

Below is a recursive function. Given a position x **in Fibonacci sequence, this method should tell you what number is at that position. However, something is wrong with this method.**

```
//precondition: x > 0

1    int fib(int x)
2        if(x ≤ 2)
3            return 1
4        else
5            return fib(x) + fib(x - 1)
6        end if
7    end fib
```

Which of the following changes would fix the method so that it works as specified?

a. replace line 5 with `return fib(x - 1) + fib(x - 2)`
b. replace line 3 with `return 0`
c. replace line 2 with `if(x < 2)`
d. replace line 5 with `return fib(x) + fib(x + 1)`

45. A dog owner designed an automatic dog feeder. When the dog pushes a button, an electronic signal triggers a motor to open a hatch and drop a treat into the dog's bowl. The dog only knows that when he pushes the button, he gets a treat. In computer science, this concept is known as __________.

a. abstraction
b. inheritance
c. polymorphism
d. aliasing

46. Use the following Java code to answer the question:

```
int array[] = {57, 32, 45, 99, 12, 6};
int lowest = 0;
for(int i = 0; i < array.length; i++)
{
	if(lowest > array[i])
	{
		lowest = array[i];
	}
}
System.out.println(lowest);
```

Which of the following should be changed in order for the code to find and print the lowest number in the `array`?

a. `if(lowest > array[i])` should be changed to `if(lowest < array[i])`
b. `lowest = array[i]` should be changed to `array[i] = lowest`
c. `int lowest = 0` should be changed to `int lowest = array[0]`
d. `for(int i = 0; i < array.length; i++)` should be changed to `for(int i = 0; i <= array.length; i++)`

47. Look at the following array sorted in ascending order.

`int[] A← [1,5,7,9,12,18,30]`

Using a binary search, what is the maximum number of iterations the search must complete to find any target number contained in the array?

a. 1
b. 7
c. 3
d. 6

48. In traditional binary storage, a ______ is a unit of measurement equal to 2^{40} bytes.

a. megabyte
b. gigabyte
c. terabyte
d. petabyte

49. Consider the algorithm below.

```
int mystery(int size, int[] list, int newValue)
      for(int i ← 0; i < size; i ← i + 1)
            if(list[i] - newValue < 0)
                  list[i] ← newValue - list[i]
            else
                  list[i] ← list[i] - newValue
            end if
      end for
end mystery
```

If we assume that `list` is not empty, that `size` represents the number of elements in `list`, and that `newValue` is an integer greater than 0, which choice best describes what this method does?

a. Replaces all values in `list` with `newValue`
b. Compares the values in `list` to `newValue` but doesn't change `list`
c. Replaces each value in `list` with the absolute value of the quantity `list[i]-newValue`
d. Changes all positive numbers in `list` to negative numbers that have the same absolute values

50. In this question, each time `spin()` is called, a number from the following wheel is returned:

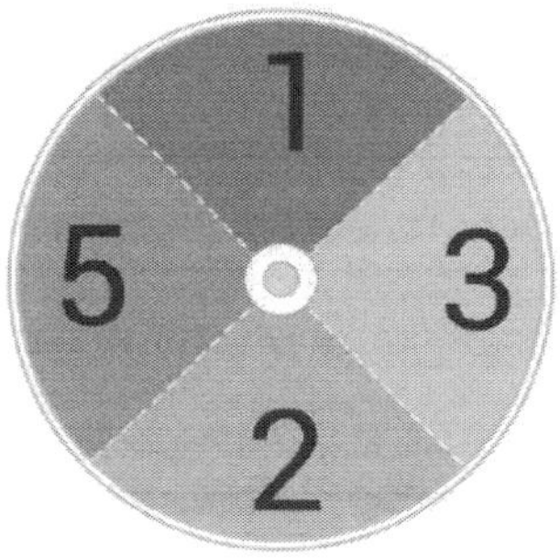

Using this code, what is the largest value of `total` that can be returned?

```
int playGame()
      int total ← 0
      total ← total + spin()
      if(total == 2)
            total ← total + 2 * spin()
      end if
      total ← total + spin()
      return total
end playGame
```

a. 12
b. 10
c. 17
d. 8

51. Given the following decision statements, which set of values for `num` represents the minimum number of test cases to ensure that the decision statement runs correctly for all valid numerical inputs?

```
if(num < 0)
{
	System.out.println("Low");
}
else if(num >= 0 && num < 10)
{
	System.out.println("Medium");
}
else if(num >= 10 && num < 20)
{
	System.out.println("High");
}
else
{
	System.out.println("Extra High");
}
```

a. 0, 5, 15
b. -5, 0, 5, 10, 15, 20, 25
c. 0, 10, 20, 30
d. -5, 0, 1, 5, 9, 10, 11, 19, 20, 21, 30

52. One of the most well-known tests in computer science is the Turing test. This test determines __________.

a. if an algorithm is the most efficient solution
b. if an AI is believable
c. the time it takes for a process to complete
d. if a network exists

53. Which of the following is an example of abstraction?

a. When I press the gas pedal, the car moves.
b. When I move the tip of a pencil across the surface of a paper, I write.
c. When I throw a ball in the air, it comes back down.
d. When I walk in the rain, I get wet.

54. Which of the following is NOT terminology that directly relates to object-oriented programming?

a. Class
b. Inheritance
c. Polymorphism
d. Syntax

55. Which of the following is an unethical use of another's intellectual property?

a. Quoting an author from their book when talking to a friend
b. Implementing the use of someone's dance move in a video game
c. Dressing like someone on TV
d. Modifying an open-source program

56. What will be printed when the following Java code runs?

```
int num = 459;
int sum = 0;

while(num > 0)
{
      sum = sum + num % 10;
      num = num / 10;
}
System.out.println(sum);
```

a. 18
b. 12
c. 0
d. 45

57. Suzie's softball team just won the championship game. She and everyone else on the team want to high five each teammate exactly once. What category of algorithm would best describe the total number of high fives for a team of size *n*?

a. Linear
b. Quadratic
c. Exponential
d. Logarithmic

58. Which of the following is NOT a means by which a consumer provides data that companies may collect?

a. Writing an email
b. Saving a text file locally
c. Using social media sites
d. Filling out online surveys

59. Which of the following is NOT a benefit of using an integrated development environment (IDE)?

a. Automatic error corrections
b. Increased efficiency
c. Possibility for collaboration
d. Readily available debugging tools

60. Jason has a program that allows the user to enter the number of hours they have exercised in the past year. It currently has a dropdown list that contains the values "1 to 10," "11 to 20," and "21+." He wants to make his program more specific, so he will replace the dropdown list with a textbox. What must he include in his code with this change?

a. A check to ensure the number entered is negative
b. A check to ensure the number entered is positive
c. A check to see if the number entered is an integer
d. A check to see if the number entered is between 1 and 21

61. Use the following Java method to answer the question:

```
public static int mystery(int[] a, int target)
{
    for(int i = 0; i < a.length; i++)
    {
        if(target == a[i])
        {
            return i;
        }
    }
    return -1;
}
```

What will this code display?

```
int[] array = {3, 5, 3, 6};
System.out.println(mystery(array, 3));
```

a. -1
b. 2
c. 3
d. 0

62. What does the following code do?

```
int go(int[] array, int size)
int temp ← 0;
        for(int j ← 0; j < size - 1; j ← j + 1)
            for(int i ← 0; i < size - 1; i ← i + 1)
                if(array[i] < array[i+1])
                    temp ← array[i]
                    array[i] ← array[i+1]
                    array[i+1] ← temp
                end if
            end for
        end for
return array[0]
end go
```

a. Sorts the array in descending order and returns the smallest number
b. Sorts the array in ascending order and returns the largest number
c. Sorts the array in descending order and returns the largest number
d. Sorts the array in ascending order and returns the smallest number

63. A robot has a light sensor that detects whether an object placed in front of it is mostly white or mostly black, using an output range from 1 to 100 where everything 50 or under is mostly white and everything from 51 to 100 is mostly black. Which of the following transformations of data would NOT make the data more readable?

a. Removing values greater than 100
b. Replacing values from 1 to 50 with "white" and replacing values from 51 to 100 with "black"
c. Rounding decimals to the nearest integer
d. Removing values less than 1

64. What will be the values of a and b after this Java code executes?

```
int a = 12;
int b = 7;
if(a > b)
      b = a + b;
if(a < b)
      a += 10;
if(a - b > 0)
{
      a++;
      b++;
}
```

a. a = 22; b = 19
b. a = 12; b = 7
c. a = 12; b = 19
d. a = 23; b = 20

65. Rick is storing color information in which each pixel can be one of eight different colors. His picture is 40px by 20px. How many bytes are needed to store his picture?

a. 6400
b. 800
c. 300
d. 2400

66. In a computer programming language's IDE, the part of the program that changes the source code into executable code is called the ________.

a. compiler
b. debugger
c. executor
d. builder

67. Convert 35_{10} to octal.

a. 43
b. 40
c. 41
d. 42

68. A company is designing a game on a 100-by-100 grid. Up to four players move around the board at the same time trying to collect coins that are randomly generated on this grid. Every time a player moves, the player object is moved one square either vertically, horizontally, or diagonally. Every time the player attempts to move, this code is executed:

```
onKeyPress()
    if(checkCollision(myPlayer, otherPlayer))
        myPlayer.stop()
    end if
end onKeyPress
```

This code should make sure that no two players are ever in the same grid box at the same time. What is a possible problem with the code?

a. The code should use a while loop.
b. Players may still collide because the code is asynchronous.
c. Players may still collide because the code is synchronous.
d. The code should use recursion.

69. What integer value for `x` will result in the variable `result` being equal to 6?

```
int x;
int result = 13 / x;
```

a. No values for `x` will calculate `result` as 6.
b. 2
c. 3
d. 4

70. Katie is designing a video game in which you can drive a car. Currently, people who are testing her game say that the driving feels too easy to control, as the car does not go off the road no matter what speed it is traveling. Which of the following will make the controls more realistic?

a. Increasing the processing power of the computer
b. Increasing the number of variables simulated
c. Decreasing the input lag
d. Decreasing the simulation detail

71. A robotics team is designing a robot that will continue to move forward at a rate of 10 cm per second until an obstacle is reached. Currently, an obstacle is positioned approximately 50 cm away. In the code below, the variable `obstacle` refers to a Boolean variable received from the sensor that detects whether there is an obstacle (true) or whether there is not an obstacle (false) in front of the robot at that point in time. The variable `forward` is a Boolean variable to determine if the robot should continue moving forward (true) or not (false). Which of the following code snippets would work best to complete this task?

a.
```
if(obstacle == false)
   forward ← true
else
   forward ← false
end if
```

b.
```
while(obstacle == true)
   forward ← false
end while
   forward ← true
```

c.
```
if(obstacle == true)
   forward ← true
else
   forward ← false
end if
```

d.
```
while(obstacle == false)
   forward ← true
end while
   forward ← false
```

72. What is a data breach?

a. Any use or viewing of files without permission
b. Any action that violates a company's security policies
c. Any violation of the Department of Homeland Security's privacy policies and procedures
d. Any observable occurrence in a system or network that has negative consequences

73. A sequence of statements in binary that is generated by compiling is called _________.

a. source code
b. object code
c. script code
d. Boolean code

74. Rachel needed to calculate the user's input raised to the 4th power. The user's input was stored in a variable named `userInput`. Instead of multiplying the variable by itself 4 times, she did the following:

```
double answer ← Math.pow(userInput, 4)
```

This function was not available in her programming language, but it was added via a widely accessible group of code. This is an example of using a ________.

a. map
b. codebase
c. repository
d. library

75. In which situation must we use lossless compression?

a. A photo file
b. A text file
c. A music file
d. A video file

76. Which of the following is a reason programmers should always document their code well?

a. The code will not work without good documentation.
b. Certain development methods require it.
c. Clarifying what the code does is often helpful.
d. Some error messages are related to improper documentation.

77. Which of the following is the defining feature of a cluster computer system?

a. It relies on redundant storage disks.
b. It uses a battery and can be held in the hand.
c. It consists of many computers working together.
d. It allows many users to compute on the same server.

78. Ping pong balls are often used in generating numbers for the lottery. When a number pops up in the machine, this number can be categorized as _________.

a. pseudorandom
b. random
c. deterministic
d. static

79. Which of the following is an example of a problem a computer will never be able to solve?

a. The halting problem
b. The traveling salesman problem
c. The Tower of Hanoi problem
d. The Turing test problem

80. Which of the following is a programming paradigm that allows the programmer to assert a desired result and does not address how to achieve the result?

a. Imperative
b. Object oriented
c. Procedural
d. Declarative

81. A student typed the following in her code segment:

```
float answer ← 17 / 3
```

What must be different about her code segment so that she always gets the correct answer?

a. The numerator should be a decimal value.
b. The denominator should be a decimal value.
c. Either the numerator or the denominator should be a decimal value.
d. Both the numerator and the denominator should be a decimal value.

82. Which of the following is NOT a factor that may prevent a computer from solving a problem?

a. time
b. storage space
c. cost
d. an infinite loop

83. Use the following Java method to answer the question:

```
public static double myMethod(double num1, double num2)
{
     double total = 1;
     for(int i = 1; i <= num1; i++)
     {
          total = total * num2;
     }
     return total;
}
```

Which expression is the equivalent of calling `myMethod(2, 3)`**?**

a. `Math.pow(2, 3);`
b. `Math.pow(3, 2);`
c. `3 * 2;`
d. `2 % 3;`

84. When the following Java code executes, what will be the values within the array `myNums`**?**

```
int[] myNums = {5, 3, 8, 1};
for(int x:myNums)
{
     x = x + 1;
}
```

a. 5, 3, 8, 1
b. 6, 4, 9, 2
c. 1, 2, 3, 4
d. 2, 3, 4, 5

85. A student writes the following code to add up the items in an array.

```
int[] nums ← [4, 9, 12, 52]
int total
for(int i ← 0; i < 4; i ← i + 1)
      total ← total + nums[i]
end for
```

The code is giving an error. Why?

a. The variable `i` should be declared before the loop.
b. The loop will be infinite.
c. `total` needs to be initialized to a value.
d. There will be an out of bounds error.

86. Trace the following code and determine the values of `a` and `b` when the code completes.

```
int mystery(int x, int y)
      if(x > y)
            y ← x - y
      else
            y ← y + x
      end else
      return y
end mystery
a ← 5
b ← 4
a ← mystery(a, b)
```

a. `a` is 1 and `b` is 4.
b. `a` is 9 and `b` is 4.
c. `a` is 5 and `b` is 4.
d. `a` is 5 and `b` is 1.

87. Which of the following is a heuristic approach to solving a problem?

a. Using an antivirus program to look for patterns common to a family of viruses
b. Using the Pythagorean theorem to solve for the longest side of a triangle
c. Planning a budget to get the highest return on investments
d. Measuring the area of a room to determine the number of floor tiles needed to cover it

88. Given the following Java class:

```
public class Rectangle
{
      int length, width;

      public Rectangle(int length, int width)
      {
      this.length = length;
      this.width = width;
      }

      public int getArea()
      {
            return length * width;
      }

      public int getPerimeter()
      {
            return 2 * length + 2 * width;
      }
}
```

What will the following code output?

```
Rectangle a = new Rectangle(3, 2);
Rectangle b = new Rectangle(3, 1);
System.out.println(Math.max(a.getArea(),
b.getPerimeter()));
```

a. 6
b. 10
c. 4
d. 8

89. Which of the following is NOT a valid debugging technique?

a. Using print statements to print out current values
b. Using watchpoints
c. Recompiling the program
d. Changing the input

90. In reviewing her lesson plans and test data following the completion of a unit, which of the following should the teacher be most concerned about regarding her students?

a. Multiple students finished the project two days before it was due, and she had to quickly create enrichment activities for them to complete so they would not become bored and distract others
b. Two lessons took longer than anticipated due to student questioning and classroom engagement
c. Several students with documented learning disabilities struggled with the unit and were unable to complete their project
d. ELL students had to use their translators and dictionaries on difficult vocabulary more than they have in the past

91. Barry wrote a program and realized that he needed to find the sum of the integers in an array. He also realized he needed to do this same operation many times in his program, so he wrote the following method:

```
int sumArray(int[] a, int size)
        int sum ← 0
        for(int i ← 0; i < size; i ← i + 1)
                sum ← sum + a[i]
        end for
end sumArray
```

Programming in this way is an example of ________.

a. extensibility
b. modifiability
c. reusability
d. testability

92. Trace the following recursive function. What is the value of `mystery(4)`?

```
int mystery(int x)
        if(x == 2 or x == 3)
                return x + mystery(x - 1)
        else if(x == 0)
                return 0
        else
                return 2 * x + mystery(x - 1)
        end else
end mystery
```

a. 8
b. 15
c. 5
d. 0

93. Which of the following is an example of bad documentation practice?

a. Leaving brief comments within the code
b. Adding images to documentation
c. Describing classes and methods
d. Giving variables arbitrary names

94. Which of the following communication mediums allows for the highest data transfer rate?

a. CAT-5
b. Fiber-optic
c. Coaxial
d. Twisted pair

95. Which of the following hardware components is responsible for drawing objects on the monitor?

a. GPU
b. CPU
c. RAM
d. ROM

96. John wants to animate a character in a video game. To do this, he needs to create a walking animation. There are many parts to this animation, so he decides to start by just making the character's leg move. This is an example of ________.

a. structural breakdown
b. abstraction
c. decomposition
d. top-down design

97. In the following Java code, how many times will the string "Incorrect." print?

```
int password = 1232;
do
{
     System.out.println("Incorrect.");
     password += 2;
} while(password <= 1234);
```

a. 0
b. 1
c. 2
d. 3

98. Aaron has just created a new software program. He wants people to be able to try it out for a month. Then, if they like it, they must pay a fee to continue using it. In order to use this method, he should offer his software as ________.

a. open-source
b. shareware
c. freeware
d. shovelware

99. Trace the following algorithm and determine the results when the input is `[2, 4, 8, 4]`**. What is printed to the screen?**

```
int x ← 5
for(int i ← 1; i < 4; i ← i + 1)
     x ← x + list[i-1]
end for
print x
```

a. 14
b. 19
c. 21
d. 16

100. The New York City subway system captures the following data on a particular route. The subway train's maximum speed is 55 miles per hour.

Day	Distance	Time
1	500 miles	1 hour
2	0 miles	0 hours
3	150 miles	3 hours

A program attempts to compute the average speed of the train for each day by dividing the distance traveled by the time it took to travel that distance. Which of the following statements is true given this scenario?

I. Either the calculation for Day 1 will cause an error or the sensor information is invalid.

II. Either the calculation for Day 2 will cause an error or the sensor information is invalid.

III. Either the calculation for Day 3 will cause an error or the sensor information is invalid.

a. I only
b. II only
c. I and II
d. I, II, and III

Answer Key and Explanations

1. B: `num ≥ 4`. Each time the recursive function is called, the number inputted as a parameter is decreased by 1. The base case is that when the number becomes 4, it will return 0 and the recursion will unwind. Therefore, any inputs that are 4 or greater will eventually trigger the base case. While `num > 4` doesn't cause infinite recursion, `num = 4` is also valid and must be included in the precondition in order to include all valid inputs.

2. B: A pie chart is the best option when trying to visualize percentages of a whole population. A bar graph could show the percentages; however, it is difficult to see how each bar corresponds to the school population as a whole. A line graph and scatter plot work better for displaying two variable data sets. For example, a line graph would work well if the school were trying to display a graph of the number of students that were present each day of school for a year.

3. D: Blue, Orange, Orange, Blue, Red, Blue, Blue. The best way to solve this problem is to draw it out and refer to the programming interface that Sarah has created. These directions make the robot move one square east, then turn 180 degrees, move back to the starting position, face north, and then move north twice.

4. A: Since there are 8 bits in a byte, the maximum size of the file is $7 \times 8 + 3 = 59$ bits. The current size is $3 \times 8 + 5 = 29$ bits. Therefore, we can calculate the remaining number of bits by subtracting 29 from 59, giving us 30 bits.

5. B: `num ≠ 0` is a necessary precondition of the given code. Since the program has the calculation `total / num`, if `num` is 0, there will be a divide-by-0 error. This could be fixed by merely changing the **`if`** statement to exclude 0, by writing **`if`**`(num > 0)`—thus removing the need for a precondition altogether.

6. B: In this scenario, ChitChat is an example of an interpreted language. Interpreted languages require a piece of software called an interpreter to read the source code and decode it so that the computer running it can understand it. Compiled languages create executable code that is already in the language that the computer can understand, so it does not need an interpreter. There is not enough information given about the language to determine if it is an object-oriented or assembly language.

7. B: Procedural programming is based on procedure calls. Object-oriented programming relies on the concepts of classes and objects. Functional programming is the process of building software by composing functions. Low-level programming is writing machine language—code that is directly executed by the CPU—or writing in a programming language that is not far removed from machine language.

8. B: When the `substring` function is given two parameters, the first parameter is the index of the character that we want to begin copying. The second parameter is one more than the last character we want to copy. Since index values start at 0, `sport.substring(1, 2)` gives only the character at index 1, which is "y". The next function, `sport.substring(3, 6)` gives the characters from index values 3 through 5, or "nas". Therefore, `b + a` concatenates, or places together, the two strings, giving "nasy" as the resulting string.

9. A: The correct order of abstraction for software from top to bottom is user, application, operating system, hardware. The user interacts with the application, which talks with the operating system, which in turn communicates with the hardware.

10. C: This program uses a for loop to look at each element of the array `words`. As it does this, it checks to see if each string begins with the capital letter C. Note that only `Claire` and `Charles` begin with a capital C. When the program finds those items, it then takes their current index value and adds it to a counter. Because arrays start with index 0, `Claire` is found at index 2, and `Charles` is found at index 3. Adding these together gives us the answer, 5.

11. B: There is an index out of bounds error. During the loop, the statement attempts to access index values of 0, 1, 2, and 3. However, index 3 is outside the bounds of the array, since there are only three items in the array, and index values start at 0. The only valid index values are 0, 1, and 2. A null pointer exception happens when you try to access an object that has not been constructed. Incompatible types happen when you try to store the value of one type of value in a different, incompatible type of variable. For example, trying to store a 4 in a Boolean variable is not possible. Missing return statement happens when a method is written that expects a return statement but one is not provided. Since this method is void, no return is expected.

12. C: David should use a hub. A hub is exactly what is needed, as it is the cheapest solution that will repeat all information that is sent to it and broadcast it to all computers that are connected to it. A gateway regulates traffic between two dissimilar networks, while a router forwards packets between different IP networks. Both have the capability to direct traffic to where it needs to go. A switch is a piece of hardware that connects devices, such as printers, to a computer using MAC addresses; however, it only directs data to a specified device, while a hub directs data to all connected devices.

13. A: Deterministic. Deterministic means that the output is predetermined by the input. Since this is the case, random numbers cannot be created by a computer. Only pseudorandom numbers can be created, through means such as measuring CPU cycles.

14. B: Creating and enacting a no-bullying policy should be one of the first steps that the classroom teacher and the resource teacher should work together on to help improve the classroom environment. This should not only educate the students on why it is inappropriate to tease the child with hearing loss but should prevent other children from being bullied in the class as well. No-bullying policies can be implemented by setting guidelines for appropriate behavior and administering consequences when bullying occurs. Correcting inappropriate behavior is a good step to take, but it is not always appropriate to punish students immediately in front of the class because it may single out students who do not understand what they are saying and how it is inappropriate. Moving the child to a self-contained environment does not allow for the least restrictive environment for the student and is not an acceptable solution. Contacting all parents and guardians to explain what is occurring in class is not a feasible solution without first trying other solutions.

15. C: The person who requested the conference should be the one who starts the conference so they are able to establish the purpose of the meeting. This could be a teacher, counselor, administrator, parent, or (in some cases) even the student. This allows everyone in attendance to know the purpose of the meeting so they are better able to focus their discussion and not waste valuable time. Administrators, school counselors, parents, and teachers can all request meetings, and if they are the ones to request the meeting, they should generally be prepared to be the ones that will open the meeting. However, it is important to note that in some instances when a parent requests a conference, it may still be best for a staff or faculty member to introduce and organize the discussion to help establish clear lines of communication.

16. C: Because the method is inside of the class, you are able to call the `getSuit()` method and `getValue()` method without putting an object in front of them. Putting the `Card` class in front of the calls for the methods is incorrect, as that would only work if the methods were static. Next, using the % operator will return the remainder after division. By checking to see if the result is 0, we are determining that the number evenly divides by 2, which is what is necessary to win the game.

17. A: To determine what values will cause the statement to evaluate to true, use a truth table:

a	b	(a && b)	!(a && FALSE)	(a && b) && !(a && FALSE)
true	true	true	true	true
true	false	false	true	false
false	true	false	true	false
false	false	false	true	false

According to the truth table, the expression only becomes true when both `a` and `b` are true.

18. C: Randomly generating a username for a new user would be a good use of randomization. Since a username's only requirement is that it cannot preexist in the database, it would be a great item for a computer to randomly generate. An item's cost and inventory should be determined by data retrieved from a database and would not make sense to be randomized. Similarly, items in a user's shopping cart are determined by the user, not by the computer.

19. C: Line 3 contains the error. In this line, Jane does not take the opportunity to use the parameters that were passed into her method. Instead, she uses literals. No matter what variables are passed in, for example `gardenArea(13.0, 15.5)`, the area will be computed using 12.5 and 14.25. Lines 1 and 2 contain errors but for different reasons than we are looking for. Line 1 is incorrect because it is returning an integer, and the result of the multiplication may be a decimal. Line 2 is incorrect because it is initializing to itself, which does not yet have a value. The error on line 4 is linked to the error on line 1 because it is trying to return a variable that is a decimal when the method is expecting to return an integer.

20. D: `Math.pow(2, 3)` means we should raise 2 to the power of 3, giving 8. We are then left with `8 + 3 * 6 - 4 * (12 - 8) / 2`. The order of operations in Java tells us that we must do parentheses first, followed by multiplication and division, followed by addition and subtraction. So, we next do the math inside the parentheses, and 12 - 8 gives us 4. We are left with `8 + 3 * 6 - 4 * 4 / 2`. Now, we do multiplication and division from left to right, giving `8 + 18 - 8`. Lastly, we complete the addition and subtraction from left to right, giving 18.

21. A: `x++` increments the value of `x` by one, giving `x = 6`.

`z--` decrements the value of `z` by 1, giving `z = 8`.

`y += z` adds the value of `z` to `y` and stores it in `y`, giving `y = 7 + 8`, or 15.

`x += x` adds the value of `x` to itself and stores it back in `x`, giving `x = 6 + 6`, or 12.

`z - y + x` gives `8 - 15 + 12`, which equals 5.

22. D: The modulo operator in Java is %. This operator returns the remainder after division. When the `mystery` method is called, 13 is passed in as the variable `a`, and 5 is passed in as the variable `b`. 13 % 5 is 3, and 5 % 13 is 5. Therefore, the else statement executes, returning `b % a`, or 5 % 13, which is 5.

23. D: Using library code is more convenient (A) and less time consuming (B). Library code is also much more likely to be bug free, having been tested by many sources. However, if you need code for a unique purpose, there may be no library functions that can directly replace your original code. In such cases, you have no choice but to write your own code

24. C: The robot will move backward, pivot right, move forward, and pivot left. Using the first input of 7 as an example, we subtract 2 from the input value to get 5. Then the modulus operator gives us the remainder after the integer division of 5 / 4, which is 1. This value maps to the command to move backward. The same procedure for the remaining inputs gives us the commands for pivot right, move forward, and pivot left. Note that for the last input, 4 – 2 gives us 2, and 2 % 4 gives us 2 as the remainder, as 4 goes into 2 zero times, with a remainder of 2.

25. A: In order to get the average of the grades, sum the grades, adding each grade to `total` as the loop executes. When that is completed, get the average by dividing the total sum by the number of grades in the array.

26. D: High-level language typically helps to deal with memory management. High-level languages are closer to human languages than computer languages. Therefore, they do not typically require the programmer to deal with problems such as memory management as much. Low-level languages are CPU-specific, provide little to no abstraction, and have almost direct communication with the hardware.

27. C: When teachers use numerous types of instructional activities, they address multiple learning needs of students in their classroom. Not all students respond well to rigid schedules, so this would not appeal to a diverse class. Simplifying content for the whole class could negatively affect higher achieving students in the class and limit the potential for growth. While learning games could increase enthusiasm, this does not target diverse learning needs.

28. B: Replace all the instances with a constant to represent the shipping cost and set it to 12. It is always the best choice to use a constant to represent information that may change in the future. If Robert had used a constant named `SHIPPING_COST` to represent the cost throughout his program, he could then just set `SHIPPING_COST ← 12`, in one line of the program. Using find and replace is very unreliable, because every instance of 10 would be replaced with 12, even if that 10 was not referring to the shipping cost, or if there were instances of those two consecutive digits in a different number such as 3105. Using a variable to represent the shipping cost doesn't make sense because variables can change during the execution of the program, and the shipping cost will not change during execution. Manually searching for instances where 10 should be 12 will most likely work, but it is very time-consuming and prone to human error.

29. D: A major reason why the base number system in computer systems is binary is because modern computers use transistors. Transistors hold a charge and can be measured to be above a certain value, which registers as a 1, or below a certain value, which registers as a 0. In early computers before transistors were invented, vacuum tubes were used in their place. Integrated circuits are electronic circuits that may include a combination of transistors, diodes, and microprocessors combined on a single chip. The central processing unit, or CPU, is the brain of the computer, which gives commands to the other parts of the computer.

30. C: Hikers logging into a global app to report bear sightings is an example of citizen science. Citizen science uses the collective strength of a community to collect and analyze data. A small team of researchers could not collect the same amount of data about a particular topic that a large community could. A single scientist also could not go through as much information as the population at large. Social media keeping track of user opinions is not citizen science because it is done without people knowing it is being done, even if the data is then used for scientific purposes.

31. B: A logic error occurs when code runs successfully but not as intended. David forgets to use parentheses so that the numbers will be added together before they are divided by 3. The parentheses are necessary because of the order of operations. The current code will divide 81 by 3 first, yielding 27. Then 57, 22, and this value of 27 will be added together. So it will run successfully, but the result will not the average that David is trying to compute, constituting a logic error.

32. A: When following the for loop, you will notice that `k = j`, and for the first outer loop `j = 4`. So, `3 * 4 - 2 = 10`. This removes choices B and D as valid answers. The inner loop continues to run, decrementing `k` each time, which produces output of 7, 4, and 1. The program then moves back to the outer loop, decrements `j`, and runs the inner loop again, producing `741` on a new line. This pattern of reproducing the previous line's output minus the first number continues until `j = 1` and the outer loop stops.

33. A: James must ask for a list of numbers, sort the numbers, ask for a target number, and then do a binary search. A binary search works only if the numbers are sorted. Also, the list must be populated first before it can be sorted.

34. B: 40 then 7 will be printed when the code is executed. The variable `cost` is used as a global variable and a local variable. The local variable of `cost` is initialized to 8 and then multiplied by `number` and returned. However, the global variable is initialized to 7 and then printed out without any other operation.

35. B: Her neighbor's Wi-Fi speed will decrease. When you sign up for internet access through your ISP, you are given a certain throughput, or speed. As more devices join the network through your wireless router and begin to transfer data, that throughput gets utilized and the speed decreases. So, if Becky decided to connect multiple devices to her neighbor's Wi-Fi, the overall internet speed would decrease drastically. Becky could not be arrested for Wi-Fi signal theft because it technically is not against the law to use it, and it is not password protected. Her neighbor's ISP would not know that Becky was using her neighbor's connection because the Wi-Fi connection is sent by the neighbor's router, not the ISP itself. Becky would not be more exposed to computer viruses than if she were using her own internet and router.

36. B: A web browser receives and sends requests between the web server and client computers. A compiler is used for taking program code and converting it into code that the computer can read. A database is used to store information, and SSL stands for secure sockets layer, which is a security layer for sending encrypted information over the internet.

37. A: When testing conditional statements, you must always test a value within the range and also at the endpoint(s). In choice A, 101 is a value within the range, 100 is at the endpoint for that range, 75 is in the second range, 50 is at the endpoint of the second range, and 25 doesn't satisfy either of the conditions, so it tests the else portion.

38. D: When the `substring` method has one parameter, the substring is the string that begins at the inputted index and runs to the end of the string. Therefore, when the loop executes, the index increments by 2 each time; `myString.substring(0)` and `myString.substring(2)` will be displayed on the same line, giving "ballll."

39. C: The idea for a better toaster could not be protected by a copyright. Copyright only protects tangible items and original works, and an idea is not tangible. A painting is the most tangible of all, so that can be copyrighted. A blueprint for a house is a tangible plan for something to be created. Computer code, while not physical in itself, does represent the creation of a computer program.

40. D: Runtime error. The variable `answer` is never given an initial valuebefore the statement `answer ← answer + 1` executes. When the program tries to use `answer`, there is no defined value stored in it yet. This problem occurs while the program is running, so it is a runtime error. A roundoff error occurs when a value loses precision, such as when a decimal is stored in an integer. A logic error occurs when the program runs but produces the wrong result. A compile-time error occurs before the program runs, such as with a syntax mistake or an undeclared variable.

41. D: Because there are only two possible values (a.m. or p.m.), a Boolean value would be most efficient. "True" could represent a.m., and "false" could represent p.m., for example. Although a string could be used, this datatype would take up more memory.

42. C: A heuristic approach is used mainly when an approximate answer is acceptable because efficiency is key. This is often the case when an answer is needed quickly because conditions are changing in real time. For example, if a person were driving (as in answer choice C), they would likely prefer to be given a "good guess" at the best route very quickly, as the alternative is to receive the perfect path but only after a relatively long wait. If the calculation takes even a little bit too long, it will no longer be valid, because the driver will have already passed that route.

43. D: A computer using a random number generator is not a truly random event. Standard computer algorithms are incapable of creating a truly random number because a computer's results are predetermined based on a certain input. The best they can do is generate a pseudorandom number by using a predetermined but ever-changing event, such as the current time in milliseconds as a seed number. The computer performs calculations based on that seed number and determines which number to generate.

44. A: Line 5 should be replaced with `return fib(x-1) + fib(x-2)`. The method must add together the two values before position `x` in order to generate the value for position `x`. Calling the function `fib(x-1)` gets the term immediately before `x`, and calling `fib(x-2)` gets the term before that.

45. A: This concept is known as abstraction. Abstraction is reducing complexity through the removal of details. The dog does not know, or care, about the inner workings of the dog feeder. His input is the press of the button, and the output is the dog treat; the mechanics behind it are hidden. Inheritance is when one object takes on characteristics of another object, usually in object-oriented programming. Polymorphism is the capability of one interface to be used for different underlying data types. Aliasing is when an object has different names that all point to the same memory address.

46. C: Setting `lowest` to 0 assumes that the smallest number in `array` will be less than or equal to 0. If all the numbers in the array were positive, 0 would remain the lowest number and would be displayed as being the smallest number even though it doesn't exist in the array. Initializing `lowest` to a number from the array, such as `array[0]`, would guarantee that a number within the array is found to be the smallest number.

47. C: 3. To answer this question, it is necessary to know how a binary search works. A binary search begins at the center of the array and continuously reduces the number of possible choices by half each iteration. The equation to determine the maximum number of iterations of a binary search is ceil($\log_2 N$), where N is the number of items in the array. The result of this calculation is 3.

48. C: When counting bytes, each prefix before "byte" represents a different multiple of 10 as the exponent of 2. From small to large, 2^0 bytes is 1 byte, 2^{10} bytes is 1 kilobyte, 2^{20} bytes is 1 megabyte, 2^{30} bytes is one gigabyte, 2^{40} bytes is one terabyte, and 2^{50} bytes is one petabyte.

49. C: The if statement checks to see if subtracting `newValue` from the item in `list` results in a negative number. If this is true, rather than subtracting from the item in `list`, the algorithm subtracts the value in `list` from `newValue`, which is inserted in `list`. The **`else`** block does the reverse (i.e., subtracts `newValue` from the item in `list` and replaces the item in `list` with this new value). This is an indirect way of finding the absolute value of the difference between two integers (in this case, `list[i]` and `newValue`).

50. C: 17 is the largest value that can be returned. The way to get the highest score is to first spin a 2. This not only adds 2 to your total but also allows you to spin again. On the next spin, whatever is spun is multiplied by 2. If you spin a 5 here, your total is now $2 + 2 \times 5 = 12$. Then you get to spin one last time, and if another 5 is spun you will get your largest possible score, which is 17.

51. B: When testing all possible bounds, you must choose one number within the bounds and one at each endpoint.

52. B: The Turing test determines if an AI is believable. Alan Turing was a computer science pioneer who developed a test to determine a computer's ability to mimic human intelligence. The test is administered by a human typing through a computer. They will either be communicating with another human or a computer, and it is up to that person to determine which it is.

53. A: When a person presses the gas pedal of a car, there are many things that go on inside the car to make it move. This is an example of abstraction because these inner workings are hidden from the driver; the driver only sees the result of the car moving. None of the other choices represent abstractions. In each case, the effect results directly from the cause, with no hidden processes.

54. D: Syntax refers to the rules of a programming language and does not directly relate to object-oriented programming. Classes are the basis of object-oriented programming because they are used to create instances of objects. Inheritance refers to one class inheriting the properties of another. Polymorphism refers to one object being represented as another object in the current context.

55. B: Implementing the use of someone's dance move in a video game illustrates an unethical use of another's intellectual property. Recently, a popular video game charged users for dance moves that were made famous by musicians and entertainers. These musicians and entertainers were not compensated by the company; therefore, it was unethical to use them. Quoting an author when talking to a friend and dressing like someone on TV is not copyright infringement and is not unethical. Also, it is not unethical to modify an open-source program because open-source programs are meant to be modified.

56. A: Each time the loop executes, `num % 10` gives you the rightmost digit of the number. This number is then added to the `sum` variable. Dividing `num` by 10 on the next line removes the digit that was just added. So, the variable `num` changes from 459 to 45 to 4 and then to 0 because of the way integer division works. Each time, the rightmost digit is added to `sum`, giving you 9 + 5 + 4 = 18.

57. B: This is an example of a quadratic algorithm. The number of high fives would be given by the equation $n \times \frac{n-1}{2}$. If you graph $y = x \times \frac{x-1}{2}$ you will get a parabola, which is a quadratic equation.

58. B: Since the text file is saved locally, the information it contains is not available for companies to collect. Social media, surveys, and emails can all be used by the company that owns them to mine for data that can then be used for advertising purposes, for example.

59. A: Although an IDE increases efficiency (B), allows for collaboration (C), and includes debugging tools (D), it does not automatically fix mistakes in code.

60. B: Because he will make the input more open-ended, Jason must now include some data validation to ensure that the user does not input invalid data. It's not possible to exercise a negative number of hours, so a check to ensure the number entered is positive would be the most appropriate. It isn't necessarily an issue if the number entered is a decimal or outside the range of 1 to 21.

61. D: This method is a search method. When it finds the target number while searching through the array from left to right, it returns the index of where it was found. If it is not found, it returns -1. Since 3 is in the first spot of the array, which is index 0, that is what is returned.

62. C: The code sorts the array in descending order and returns the largest number. The sort used in this example is a bubble sort. Each element is compared to its neighbor. In this case, if the left item is smaller than the right item, their positions are switched. This results in the array being sorted from greatest to least. Lastly, the `return array[0]` returns the leftmost item in the array, which at this point will be the largest number.

63. C: Rounding decimals to the nearest integer would not make the data more readable. Rounding decimals to integers does not make them more readable in this example, as you will still have to figure out if the resulting value is both within the acceptable range and if it should be interpreted as black or white. Removing values less than 1 and greater than 100 gets rid of values that are outside of the acceptable range, so this makes sense. Replacing values from 1 to 50 with white and 51 to 100 with black also makes sense because it will be easier to read which objects are black and which are white.

64. D: The first if statement `(12 > 7)` is true, so `b = 12 + 7`, or 19. Then, `(12 < 19)` is also true, so `a` gets incremented by 10, giving `a = 22`. Lastly, 22 – 19 = 3, which is greater than 0, so `a` and `b` both increase by 1, giving `a = 23` and `b = 20`. All three if statements execute because they are stand-alone if statements, and they do not have if-else clauses attached.

65. C: 300 bytes are needed to store his pictures. To find the solution, you must first realize that to represent 8 different colors, you need 3 bits because $2^3 = 8$. With 3 bits, you can map to a maximum of 8 different values. Since there are 3 bits per pixel, you multiply that by the length and width of the picture, which gives you $3 \times 40 \times 20 = 2400$ bits. Since we want the answer in bytes, we then must divide by 8, as there are 8 bits in a byte. The final answer is then 300.

66. A: A compiler is the part of the program that changes the source code into executable code. The compiler takes the computer code that is written by the programmer and changes it into a language that the computer can understand. A debugger is a tool that helps to remove errors from the code before it runs. An executor is what runs the code. A builder is a tool that helps to automate the software creation process.

67. A: Since the octal numeral system is base 8, converting a number in base 10 to octal can be achieved by repeated division by 8. Start by dividing 35 by 8. The result is 4, with a remainder of 3. Then divide 4 by 8. The result is 0, with a remainder of 4. Since we have reached 0, we can now arrange the remainders in reverse order of how we got them. This yields the answer, 43.

68. B: Players may still collide because the code is asynchronous. In event-driven programs, such as games where players are all moving at the same time, asynchronous events occur in which one player's code could be running at the same time as another player's code. If both players check if a square is empty at the same time and then move to that same square, they will end up occupying the same square. Synchronous programming runs in order and waits until one instruction is completed before running another. The code should not use a `while` loop or recursion because the grid square is only checked each time that the `onKeyPress()` event happens.

69. B: When 13 is divided by 2, integer division occurs because both values are integers. To determine the number that is returned when doing integer division, perform normal division and drop the decimal values. In this example, 13 divided by 2 is 6.5, but because of integer division, the result is 6.

70. B: Increasing the number of variables simulated would make the controls more realistic. If the car is sticking to the road too much, the simulation needs more information to determine the correct physics based on factors such as the car's speed, trajectory, tires, and weight. This requires an increase in the number of variables in the simulation.

71. D: This answer is correct because it allows the robot to continue to move forward as long as the path ahead is free of obstacles. The other **`while`** statement in B will not work because once the **`while`** loops end, the robot will move forward forever. Neither **`if`** statements work because an **`if`** statement only checks things once and will not allow the robot to move more than a short amount of time.

72. A: Viewing or using files without permission is considered a data breach, no matter how minor the activity is. Many company data breaches happen due to database security flaws and can affect millions of people. A violation of a company's security policy (B) is called a "security incident." A violation of the Department of Homeland Security's privacy policies and procedures (C) is called a "privacy incident." An observable occurrence in a system or network that has negative consequences (D) is referred to as an "adverse event."

73. B: Object code is the sequence of binary statements that is generated by a compiler. It is usually specific to the current system architecture. For example, a Windows-based computer could not read object code intended for a Mac-based computer. Source code (A) is program code written in a programming language, and it must be compiled in order to run. Script code (C), or scripts, are series of instructions that are interpreted at runtime rather than compiled. Boolean (D) is not a type of code. In programming, the term "Boolean" most often refers to variables of the Boolean datatype, which can only be two different values ("true" or "false").

74. D: This is an example of a library. A library is a useful collection of functions that can be easily added to a program for increased functionality.

75. B: Lossless compression must be used for text files because no amount of information loss can be tolerated in text. Photos, videos, and music can all be reduced in quality through lossy compression. The loss will be acceptable since the final compressed file is still readable, and the user can still view the content.

76. C: One of the reasons why programmers should document their code well is to clarify what the code actually does. This saves time and potential confusion when others read the code, and it can serve as a much-needed reminder for the programmer if they need to access their code later on, after they've forgotten about it. Documentation is not required for the code to compile (choices A and D). In fact, the compiler completely ignores all comments. Documentation might be required by a method of development (B), but such a requirement would not be a reason to document well all the time.

77. C: Though a cluster is viewed as a single system, it utilizes networking to aggregate the computing power of many computers to work together on extremely large computing tasks. Some computers do have redundant storage disks running in parallel (A), but this is not an attribute of cluster computer systems specifically. Hand-held computers (B) have had many forms but are different from cluster computer systems. Today, it is easy to compute on the same server as other users (D), though in the past this was the function of workstations.

78. B: Ping pong balls in a lottery machine give a truly random number, as the ball that pops up is not based on any predetermined value. Pseudorandom numbers (A) are generated based on a seed value and therefore are not truly random. Deterministic numbers (C) have a predetermined value that is based on an event or equation. Static numbers (D) stay the same.

79. A: The halting problem is a problem in computer science where the goal is to determine if a program will finish running or run forever (as by getting stuck in an infinite loop). This problem is impossible for a computer to solve. The traveling salesman problem (B) can be solved by "brute force." The problem that is central to the Tower of Hanoi puzzle (C) can be solved with recursion, and the Turing test (D) has been passed by computers using AI.

80. D: There are two main programming paradigms: imperative and declarative. Imperative languages include object-oriented programming and procedural programming. These types of languages require the programmer to provide instructions to the computer on how to achieve desired results. Declarative programming is not concerned with how the computer is achieving the results, but it requires the programmer to clearly define what those results are.

81. C: With the line of code as it is, `answer` will be 5.000000 because the division that took place was integer division. In order to force decimal division, either the numerator or the denominator must be a decimal value. If decimal division is forced, `answer` will be 5.666667.

82. C: The cost of computer components is not a direct factor that will prevent a computer from solving a problem. No computer component costs an infinite amount of money. Time (A) is a factor because the problem may take an infinite amount of time. Some problems may also involve an infinite amount of space (B). Also, if a computer is ever caught in an infinite loop, it will never stop and will therefore never solve the problem.

83. B: This method repeatedly multiplies `num2` by itself, `(num1)` times. Notice the parameters are sent to the method in a different order than `Math.pow()`. Since `num1` equals 2, and `num2` equals 3, this would be the same as `Math.pow(3, 2)`, which raises 3 to the power of 2.

84. A: When using an enhanced for loop, the variable `x` is a temporary variable. That means any values added to it are lost after each iteration. Using an enhanced loop is typically not a good idea if you want to change the values of an array. It is generally the most useful when accessing every value in an array.

85. C: Notice that the line `total ← total + nums[i]` doesn't contain a declaration of the variable `total`. This variable is declared in the second line of the code. However, it should be initialized to a value when it is declared. Though a calculation itself can be the initial value of a variable, a calculation cannot be made with an uninitialized variable.

86. A: The value of `a` is 1 and the value of `b` is 4. When the method `mystery` is called, 5 is passed in as `x` and 4 is passed in as `y`. Since 5 > 4, the code `y ← x - y` is run, resulting in 1 for `y`. Then `y` is returned to the value `a` in this line, `a ← mystery(a, b)`, making `a` equal to 1. The variable `b` is left unchanged.

87. A: An antivirus program looking for patterns common to a family of viruses. A heuristic approach uses solutions that are often not perfect but good enough given time constraints. It would take a very long time to search every line of code in a program for an exact match of an existing virus, and in some cases, slight alterations to the virus wouldn't show up. Looking for generalized patterns may give some false negatives but will detect a larger group of positive virus programs as well. Answers B, C, and D can all be calculated using deductive reasoning and give answers based on a predictable set of steps.

88. D: The code creates two `Rectangle` objects, one with a `length` of 3 and `width` of 2, and one with a `length` of 3 and a `width` of 1. The code then gets the area of `Rectangle a`, which is 6, and the perimeter of `Rectangle b`, which is 8. Then, these objects interact with the `Math` class to determine which value is larger, using the `Math.max()` function. Because 8 is greater than 6, 8 is displayed.

89. C: Recompiling the program is not a valid debugging technique. Recompiling the program without any changes will not give you different results and will not help you determine any errors in the program. Using print statements will allow you to see the values of variables at different points in the program. Similarly, watchpoints will show you those values in the debugger. Changing the input may also help because certain inputs may produce errors while others may not.

90. C: The teacher should be most concerned that several students in her classroom struggled with an assignment so much that they were unable to complete it. When something like this happens in the classroom, a teacher should be willing to self-assess what they may have done incorrectly, or what they could do differently in the future. A teacher should ensure that activities and assignments in their classroom are able to be completed by all students in their classroom, even if some students may need some accommodations due to disabilities or other limitations. The goal of education is to make learning accessible for all students, and that should be one of a teacher's most important goals in the classroom.

91. C: Programming in this way is an example of reusability. Since Barry is using the code in multiple areas of his program, it is a better idea to create a method than to repeat the same code in each different area. Extensibility refers to the ability of a program to be extended and built on. An example of this is when one class inherits the capabilities of another. Modifiability is the ability for a system to be easily modified when necessary. Testability is the ability for a program to be broken down into easily testable parts.

92. B: 15. When `x` is 4 and 1, the method multiplies `x` by 2 and then adds it to the total. When it is 3 or 2, it just adds `x` to the total. The result is $4 \times 2 + 3 + 2 + 1 \times 2 = 15$.

93. D: Part of good documentation is giving variables suitable names. For example, if a variable represents the number of students in a classroom, `numStudents` would be a better variable name than `x`. If the variable names reflect the purposes of the variables, the code will be not only more readable but easier to understand in context.

94. B: Fiber-optic cables transmit data as a stream of light that flows through fibers. This is faster than the electrical signals that flow through the other three types of cables mentioned.

95. A: The GPU, or graphics processing unit is responsible for drawing objects on the monitor. The GPU is responsible for all graphics processing, including rendering the image on the screen. CPU stands for central processing unit; it is the brains of the computer and responsible for processing commands. The RAM, or random-access memory, and ROM, or read-only memory, are memory chips used to store programs that run on the computer.

96. C: This is an example of decomposition. Decomposition is the process of breaking down large problems into smaller ones. Before John can make the character have a full walk cycle, he first needs to do a simpler task, which is making his character move its leg.

97. C: A do loop will do the code contained within the body of the "do" first and then test the value of the variable after. In this way, "Incorrect." is printed first without any check. Then, `password` is incremented by 2, giving 1234. Since the loop continues while `password <= 1234`, the loop happens again. "Incorrect." is printed a second time, and `password` is now 1236. Now that `password` is no longer less than or equal to 1234, the loop terminates.

98. B: Aaron should offer his software as shareware. Shareware refers to any software that is free to begin with but becomes pay-to-use after a certain time, as designated by the creator. It is a great way for programmers to allow end users to try software before they fully commit to buying it. Open-source is any software whose source code is available to the public to view or change as they please. Freeware is software that is inherently free and will never have a price tag attached to it. Shovelware is usually lower-quality or low-value software that is bundled together with many other programs of the same type to increase its overall value.

99. B: 19. The **`for`** loop begins with `i` at 1, and each time it adds the previous item to `x`. Since `x` is initialized to 5, the resulting calculation is $5 + 2 + 4 + 8$. The last 4 in the array is never accessed because at that time `i` is equal to `4` and the loop ends.

100. C: Statement I is true because the sensor information for Day 1 must be invalid. The maximum speed of the subway train is 55 mph, and dividing 500 miles by 1 hour gives 500 mph. This means there must have been an error in the sensor information. Statement II is true because the data for Day 2 indicates that the train traveled 0 miles in 0 hours. This data is not necessarily invalid, as it is possible that the train did not run at all that day. However, the program will divide 0 by 0 to determine the speed. The division by zero will result in an error. Day 3's data seems possible, and because 150 / 3 is 50, the resulting average speed is well within the maximum speed of 55 mph.

Online Resources

Due to our efforts to try to keep this book to a manageable length, we've created a link that will give you access to all of your online resources:

mometrix.com/resources719/texescompsci241

It's Your Moment, Let's Celebrate It!

Share your story @mometrixtestpreparation